MW00694726

Devdutt Pattanaik is a medical doctor by education, a leadership consultant by profession and a mythologist by passion. He has written and lectured extensively on the nature of sacred stories, symbols and rituals and their relevance in modern times. His books with Penguin India include *The Book of Ram*, *Myth=Mithya: Decoding Hindu Mythology*, *The Pregnant King*, *Jaya: An Illustrated Retelling of the Mahabharata*, *Sita: An Illustrated Retelling of the Ramayana*, and the Devlok series of stories for children. Devdutt's unconventional approach and engaging style are evident in his lectures, books and articles. To know more visit www.devdutt.com.

By the same author

Myth=Mithya: Decoding Hindu Mythology
The Pregnant King
Jaya: An Illustrated Retelling of the Mahabharata
Sita: An Illustrated Retelling of the Ramayana
Shikhandi and Other Tales They Don't Tell You

DEVDUTT PATTANAIK

THE BOOK OF RAM

Illustrations by the author

PENGUIN BOOKS

PENGUIN BOOKS

Published by the Penguin Group

Penguin Books India Pvt. Ltd, 7th Floor, Infinity Tower C, DLF Cyber City, Gurgaon 122 002, Haryana, India

Penguin Group (USA) Inc., 375 Hudson Street, New York, New York 10014, USA

Penguin Group (Canada), 90 Eglinton Avenue East, Suite 700, Toronto, Ontario, M4P 2Y3, Canada

Penguin Books Ltd, 80 Strand, London WC2R 0RL, England

Penguin Ireland, 25 St Stephen's Green, Dublin 2, Ireland (a division of Penguin Books Ltd)

Penguin Group (Australia), 707 Collins Street, Melbourne, Victoria 3008, Australia

Penguin Group (NZ), 67 Apollo Drive, Rosedale, Auckland 0632, New Zealand

Penguin Books (South Africa) (Pty) Ltd, Block D, Rosebank Office Park, 181 Jan Smuts Avenue, Parktown North, Johannesburg 2193, South Africa

Penguin Books Ltd, Registered Offices: 80 Strand, London WC2R 0RL, England

First published by Penguin Books India 2008
This edition published 2015

Text copyright © Devdutt Pattanaik 2008
Illustrations copyright © Devdutt Pattanaik 2008

ISBN 9780143424604

Typeset in Book Antiqua by Manipal Digital Systems, Manipal
Printed at Replika Press Pvt. Ltd, India

A PENGUIN RANDOM HOUSE COMPANY

Contents

Foreword

Any discussion of Ram today is dominated either by academic analysis or political debate. The former thrives on portraying Ram as a patriarchal poet's fantasy. The latter either asserts Ram or rejects Ram, transforming him into a potent political lever either way. In the din of these discourses of power, the discourse of love is lost. One forgets that for hundreds of years, for millions of people, across history and geography, Ram's name and Ram's story has been a window to the divine.

Ram's name, the Ram-nam, is repeatedly chanted to tide over a crisis, for the name, Ram, when reversed becomes Mara, which means 'die'. Ram is the opposite of Mara. Ram is life—with all its demands and desires and destinies. Ram's calm repose in the face of all adversity, so evident in the *Ramayana*, has made him worthy of veneration, adoration and worship.

Ram's story has reached the masses not through erudite Sanskrit texts but through theatre, song and dance performed in local languages. All of these retellings of the *Ramayana* have their own twists and turns, their own symbolic outpouring, each one valid in their respective contexts.

I write this book celebrating the Ram of the common man, the power of his name, the many retellings of his tale, drawing attention to the several layers of metaphors and meanings in the rituals and narratives, bringing forth my own creative insight, well aware that:

Within infinite myths lies the Eternal Truth
Who sees it all?
Varuna has but a thousand eyes
Indra, a hundred
And I, only two

Devdutt Pattanaik

1

Ramayana's Protagonist

O beloved son of Kaushalya,
Dawn is about to break,
O lion amongst men,
Be pleased to open your eyes.
And perform the duties of the day

—From *Venkatesa Suprabhatam*
by Prathi Vadhi Bhayangaram Annangaracharyar

An upright hero

The *Ramayana,* one of the most revered texts in Hinduism, tells the story of a prince called Ram.

Dashratha, king of Ayodhya, had three wives but no children. So he conducted a yagna and invoked the gods who gave him a magic potion that was divided amongst his three queens. In time the queens gave birth to four sons. Ram was the eldest, born of the chief queen, Kaushalya, Bharata was the second, born to Dashratha's favourite queen, Kaikeyi and Lakshman and Shatrughna were the twin sons of the third queen, Sumitra.

Ram completed his early education under the tutelage of Rishi Vasishtha. He was then asked to defend Rishi Vishwamitra's hermitage from attacks by the demons known as Rakshasas.

Accordingly, Ram killed many Rakshasas in the time that he spent under Rishi Vishwamitra's care including a female Rakshasa called Tadaka. Pleased with his actions, Vishwamitra taught him many potent magical chants that transformed ordinary arrows into potent missiles.

Vishwamitra then took Ram to Mithila, capital of the kingdom of Videha. On the way, they came to the hermitage of Gautam, who had cursed his wife Ahalya to turn into stone because she had been unfaithful to him. Ram placed his foot on the stone that was Ahalya and she was instantly released from the curse, such was the purity of Ram's character.

At Mithila, Ram participated in the swayamvar being held by Janaka, the king of Videha. The young prince broke the mighty bow of Shiva that was in the king's custody and by this display of strength, won the hand of Janaka's daughter, Sita, in marriage. Sita was no ordinary woman. She had been ploughed out of the earth by Janaka who had then raised her as his own daughter.

On Ram's return to Ayodhya, Dashratha decided it was time to pass on the crown to Ram and retire from worldly life.

Devdutt Pattanaik

Unfortunately, on the eve of Ram's coronation, the maid, Manthara, poisoned Kaikeyi's mind against the coronation. Thus influenced, Kaikeyi demanded that her husband grant her the two boons he had promised her years ago when she had saved his life in battle. As her first boon, she wanted her son, Bharata, to be crowned king and for the second, she wanted Ram to live as a hermit in the forest for fourteen years.

Bound by his word, Dashratha sent for Ram and informed him of the situation. Without any remorse or regret, to the amazement of all, Ram removed his royal robes and left the city of Ayodhya dressed in clothes of bark, as hermits are supposed to, armed only with his bow.

Despite protests, Ram's wife, Sita, and his brother, Lakshman, followed him to the forest; Sita, because she refused to leave her husband's side and Lakshman, because he could not bear to be parted from his brother. Watching the three leave the city, overwhelmed by the calamity befalling his household, Dashratha died of a broken heart.

Much to Kaikeyi's disappointment, her son, Bharata, refused to take a kingdom obtained through such trickery. He decided to live as a hermit too, outside the city gates in the village of Nandigram and serve as Ram's regent until Ram's return. He placed Ram's footwear on the throne to proclaim Ram's undisputed kingship.

In the forest, Ram, Lakshman and Sita endured the vagaries of nature stoically. Wandering from place to place, through dense forests and over high hills, they never stopped at any one place for too long. Sometimes they took shelter in caves and at others they built themselves little huts using leaves and twigs. Often they fought demons who harassed them and encountered sages such as Atri and Agastya who showered them with gifts and wise words. So passed thirteen years.

In the fourteenth year of exile, a woman called Surpanakha saw Ram in the forest. Smitten by his beauty, she openly expressed her desire to be his lover. Ram politely refused on grounds that he already had a wife. Lakshman also turned her down as his only desire in life was to serve his brother and his sister-in-law.

Surpanakha blamed Sita for this rejection and tried to kill her. Lakshman rushed to Sita's rescue. Raising his sword he cut Surpanakha's nose and drove her away.

Devdutt Pattanaik

Surpanakha, who was in fact a female Rakshasa ran to her brother, Ravana, who was the ten-headed king of the Rakshasas. When the demon-king saw his sister's mutilated face, he was furious. He swore to teach Ram a lesson by abducting Sita and forcing her to be part of his vast harem.

At Ravana's behest, a shape-shifting demon called Maricha took the form of a golden deer and enchanted Sita who begged Ram to catch it for her. Ram pursued the deer and was drawn deep into the woods. When struck by Ram's arrows, Maricha shouted for help mimicking Ram's voice so perfectly that a frightened Sita ordered Lakshman to rush to Ram's rescue.

With no one around to protect Sita, Ravana approached her in the guise of a sage and asked for some food. Sita stretched out her hand and offered whatever she had in the house, taking care not to cross the line marked out by Lakshman around the hut; so long as she stayed within the line, Lakshman had said, she would be under Ram's protection and hence safe.

Ravana, however, displayed mock fury at the way the food was being offered to a sage, forcing

Sita to step out. Ravana immediately revealed his true identity, grabbed Sita, leapt on to his flying chariot and made his way across the sky to his island-kingdom of Lanka.

The two brothers returned to an empty hut after killing Maricha. Nearby was the vulture called Jatayu who had been mortally wounded while trying to stop Ravana's chariot. Before dying, Jatayu informed Ram that Ravana had carried Sita somewhere to the south. On learning of his beloved's fate, Ram was overwhelmed by grief.

Determined to rescue Sita, Ram and Lakshman made their way south. They passed the terrifying forests of Dandaka, crossed the Vindhya mountains and eventually reached Kishkindha, the land of monkeys, where they met Sugriva, a monkey who had been driven into exile by his brother, Vali, king of monkeys, following a misunderstanding.

Ram and Sugriva came to an agreement: if Ram helped overpower Vali, Sugriva would help rescue Sita. On Ram's advice, Sugriva challenged Vali to a duel. Sugriva was no match for his much stronger brother and would surely have been killed had Ram not raised his bow and shot Vali from behind the bushes while the two brothers were fighting. A dying Vali accused Ram of being unfair to which Ram retorted that those who live by the law of the jungle must allow themselves to be killed by the law of the jungle.

After becoming king, Sugriva asked all the monkeys of Kishkindha to go in every direction in search of Sita. After a long search, the strongest and wisest of all the monkeys, whose name was Hanuman, learnt from another vulture called Sampati that Ravana's kingdom, Lanka, stood in the middle of the vast ocean that stretched beyond the southern horizon. Hanuman increased his size and leapt across the sea, surviving many dangers along the way, and made his way into the island of demons. There he found Sita sitting forlorn in a palace orchard, under the Ashoka tree, rejecting Ravana's amorous advances, totally convinced that her husband would eventually come to her rescue.

As soon as she was alone, Hanuman approached Sita, identified himself, gave her Ram's ring as proof of his identity and assured her that Ram was truly on his way. Overjoyed, Sita blessed Hanuman and gave him her hairpin as proof of her discovery.

Hanuman then let himself be caught by Ravana's guards. Identifying himself as Ram's messenger, he warned Ravana with dire consequences if he did not let Sita go. Ravana laughed and ordered his guards to set Hanuman's tail on fire. No sooner was his tail set alight than Hanuman jumped free and ran amok in Lanka setting buildings on fire. He then leapt across the sea, returned to Kishkindha and revealed Sita's exact whereabouts to Ram.

Hanuman helped Ram raise a vast army of monkeys, bears and vultures. Together they built a bridge across the sea to Lanka.

As the bridge was being constructed, Ram got help from an unexpected quarter: Vibhishana, Ravana's younger brother, decided to join forces with Ram after being evicted from Lanka for publicly declaring that Ravana was morally wrong to keep a married woman in his palace against her will.

At long last, the bridge was built and Ram found himself on the shores of Lanka with his army behind him separated from Sita by the formidable walls of Ravana's citadel.

All attempts for a peaceful resolution were rejected by Ravana who felt it beneath his dignity to even consider proposals made by a man with a monkey army. War was finally declared. On one side stood Ram, Lakshman, Vibhishana, Sugriva, Hanuman and other denizens of the forest. On the other stood Ravana and his demon hordes. The monkeys fought with sticks and stones and the demons with weapons and magic. The battle was long and fierce with terrible casualties on both sides.

Lakshman was hit by a lethal arrow shot by Ravana's son, Indrajit, and would have died had Hanuman not flown north and brought back the mountain of magical herbs. Hanuman also rescued the two brothers from the sorcerer, Mahiravana.

Eventually the battle turned in Ram's favour. Ravana lost many of his sons including Indrajit. He even lost his brother, Kumbhakarna, a giant, who had been roused from his long slumber and sent to battle.

Finally, Ravana came face to face with Ram. A long duel ensued with the two showering powerful missiles at each other. Ram soon realized that Ravana had the power to replace his heads and Ram's efforts to overpower and kill him would be futile if he did not unlock the secret of the demon-king's apparent invincibility. Vibhishana then revealed to Ram that Ravana's life rested within his navel and he thus could not be slain by beheading. Ram immediately released a deadly arrow that punctured Ravana's navel and killed him instantly. As Ravana fell, the monkeys cheered. A victorious Ram declared Vibhishana king of Lanka.

It was time for Ram and Sita to be reunited. When Sita, released from her prison, approached Ram, he demanded that she prove to the world that she had been a faithful wife during her stay in Ravana's palace. Sita, startled by even the suggestion of infidelity, walked through fire. Protected by the power of her chastity, Sita emerged from the fire unscathed.

At the end of this ordeal, Ram, Lakshman and Sita returned home to Ayodhya on Ravana's flying chariot accompanied by Hanuman who accepted Ram as his lord and master. The fourteen years of exile were at an end.

The residents of Ayodhya, including Bharata, rejoiced when they saw Ram. Great celebrations followed the coronation of Ram which was attended not only by sages and gods but also by monkeys and demons. The joy was doubled when Sita declared a few months later that she was pregnant.

Not long after this happy occasion, Ram heard that his subjects gossiped about Sita's stay in Ravana's palace; they did not want a woman of soiled reputation as their queen. A heartbroken Ram ordered Lakshman to take Sita to the forest and leave her there. Lakshman obeyed with great reluctance. Abandoned for no fault of hers, Sita took shelter in the hermitage of the poet-sage Valmiki where she gave birth to twins, Luv and Kush, and raised them on her own.

Despite his personal loss, Ram ruled his kingdom diligently. His reign was so perfect that the rains came on time and no accidents ever took place. Everything was predictable and rhythmic. There was peace and prosperity in every direction.

Years later, Ram was advised to conduct the Ashwamedha yagna so that Ram's rule could spread around the world. The royal horse would be allowed to travel freely across the world; all the lands it traversed unchallenged would come under

Ram's suzerainty. But to perform this ambitious ritual, it was necessary for the patron to have a wife. With Sita gone, the people of Ayodhya asked Ram to marry again. Ram refused to do so. He had abandoned the queen his people did not want but not his wife. So he had a golden effigy of Sita made, which was placed by his side when he conducted the ritual.

The royal horse was let loose. Following it was Ram's army led by Lakshman and Hanuman. When the horse entered Valmiki's hermitage, Sita's sons caught hold of it and refused to let it go, thereby challenging Ram's authority. A great battle followed in which the two young boys were able to defeat Lakshman, Hanuman and all of Ram's soldiers without much effort. Finally Ram himself challenged the two boys to a fight. Tragedy was averted when Sita intervened and introduced her sons to her husband.

It was clear that Sita's children defeated Ram's army because righteousness rested with Sita and not with the kingdom of Ayodhya that had rejected her. Ram begged Sita to prove her chastity once more, this time before his subjects, so that the stain on her reputation was wiped off forever and she could take her rightful place beside him as queen.

Sita, tired of her character being questioned repeatedly, begged the earth to take her into its folds if she had truly been a faithful wife. Instantly the earth split open and Sita disappeared under the ground. The people of Ayodhya now had their proof but it came at the price of Ram losing his wife.

Unable to live on earth without his beloved, Ram decided to renounce his mortal body. Passing on the crown of his forefathers to his children, he walked into the Sarayu river and never rose again.

A few authors project Ram as an ordinary man who did extraordinary things, triumphing in life against all odds to become a hero first and then a god. But for his devotees he is the most perfect earthly manifestation of God to be worshipped for one's salvation.

Every year, the day of Ram's birth is celebrated in spring (Ram Navami) while the day of his triumph and his coronation are celebrated in autumn

(Dusshera and Diwali). In temples, he is the only deity to be enshrined as a king. When times are difficult, one is advised to read his tale because his uprightness in the face of all adversities offers hope and peace to all.

Devdutt Pattanaik

2

Dashratha's Son

Then he appeared

The merciful one

The benefactor of the weak

And Kaushalya was blessed

The mother beamed

Sages were unable to describe his beauty

Bewitching eyes

Dark skin

Four armed

With a garland of flowers

And large eyes, reflecting the beauty of the oceans

With folded hands we pray

O Infinite One

How does one worship you?

Do we praise your deeds?

Or do we recite the scriptures?

—From *Bhaye Prakat Kripala* of the sixteenth-century saint Tulsidas

Between destiny and desire

Before Ram, Dashratha had a daughter by Kaushalya. Her name was Shanta. Shanta's story is not found in Valmiki's *Ramayana* but can be pieced together from bits of information scattered across the *Mahabharata* and other regional retellings of Ram's tale.

Rishyashringa's curse

Angry with the clouds that had released rain and made him wet, a Rishi called Rishyashringa forbade the clouds from releasing any more rain. Rishyashringa could do this because he practiced tapasya, or absolute restraint of the senses, which included celibacy. In fact, so intense was his tapasya, that he had never seen a woman in his entire life. The resulting tapa or spiritual heat that he generated gave him siddhi or magical powers with which he could subvert the laws of nature. The only way to put an end to the drought that followed Rishyashringa's curse was to get him married. 'So long as he has no knowledge of women, the drought will continue,' the gods told a local king called Lompada. But Lompada had no daughter who could turn this hermit into a householder. So he turned to Dashratha, king of Ayodhya, who allowed Lompada to adopt his daughter, Shanta. Succeeding in arousing Rishyashringa's curiosity, Shanta made him her husband and with that the rains returned to Lompada's kingdom once more.

The story of Shanta and Rishyashringa is significant because it transforms the *Ramayana* into a householder's epic. It does not look down upon the material world. In fact, it frowns upon monastic practices that reject all things worldly.

The world may be ever-changing and full of uncertainties, but walking away is not the answer. World-rejection, according to the epic, is dangerous and destructive. That is why the rains fall and the earth blooms only when Rishyashringa embraces a woman and becomes a husband. It is this stance of the *Ramayana* that has led to its classification as iti-hasa which literally translated means 'so-it-was, is and will be'. The *Ramayana* reflects on the problem of the human condition, of how desire and destiny make the world impermanent and tragic. It also offers the solution by showing us how to live a spiritually fulfilled life through responsible conduct.

Though Dashratha seems to have fathered Shanta without any difficulty, he is unable to father any more children. Dharma insists that a man must father a son and continue his lineage and that a king must produce an heir for the throne. A desperate Dashratha therefore marries a second and a third time. When despite his numerous marriages he remains bereft of a male heir, he decides to perform a yagna and compel the gods to give him a child to carry the line of the solar-kings forward. The Rishi who is called to perform the yagna is none other than Rishyashringa, subtly implying that the Rishi's tapasya not only caused the drought in Lompada's kingdom, but also the barrenness in Dashratha's household. Rishyashringa's yagna gives sons to Dashratha, just as his marriage gave rains to Lompada.

Three wives and a yagna

Kaushalya was Dashratha's first wife. After bearing him a daughter, Shanta, she gave birth to no more children. So Dashratha married Kaikeyi, princess of Kekaya. It was foretold that Kaikeyi would bear a great son and her father gave her hand in marriage to Dashratha only after Dashratha promised that Kaikeyi's son would be his heir. Unfortunately, Kaikeyi did not bear any children, let alone sons. Finally, Dashratha married a third time. But even the third queen, Sumitra, bore no children. A frustrated and desperate Dashratha decided to perform a yagna that would please the Devas and compel them to give him a son, one who would follow him to the throne. So, the sage Rishyashringa was invited and he performed an elaborate yagna. As the yagna drew to a close, a celestial being rose from the fire-pit. Dark and dressed in red, he offered Dashratha a vessel containing a celestial potion. 'Offer this to your wives and they will bear divine sons,' said the being before disappearing. A very happy Dashratha, immediately rushed to his wives and divided the magic potion between his senior queen, Kaushalya, and his favourite queen, Kaikeyi. Both of them divided their share and gave one half each to Sumitra, the junior queen. As a result, the three queens gave birth to four sons. Vasishtha named Kaushalya's son, Ram, Kaikeyi's son, Bharata, and Sumitra's twins, Lakshman and Shatrughna. Lakshman born from the share given by Kaushalya to Sumitra grew up devoted to Ram while Shatrughna born from the share given by Kaikeyi to Sumitra grew up devoted to Bharata.

The yagna represents Dashratha's refusal to surrender to a childless fate and is a choreographed expression of Dashratha's intense desire to be a father. The *Ramayana* thus reveals a potent force governing samsara—kama or desire. Desire transforms Rishyashringa from hermit to householder. Desire causes rain to fall. Desire makes Dashratha a father.

But while desire is necessary, it is also destructive. It is desire that makes Dashratha give two boons to his favourite queen, the beautiful Kaikeyi, which results in the exile of Ram. The entire *Ramayana* anchors itself on the story of Dashratha offering Kaikeyi two boons. Had this not happened, there would have been no exile of Ram, no abduction of Sita and no war with Ravana. Ram would have been just one of the many kings of the illustrious Surya-vamsa or solar dynasty.

Two boons

On the eve of Ram's coronation, Dashratha learnt that his favourite queen Kaikeyi had locked herself in the chamber of despair. He rushed to her side and found her wailing, rolling on the ground, hair unbound, bereft of flowers and jewels. 'Give me the two boons you promised me long ago,' she said. 'Make my son, Bharata, king of Ayodhya and order Ram to live as a hermit in the forest for fourteen years.'

Why does Dashratha give Kaikeyi this boon in the first place? Was it just a whim, the desire to please his beloved, or a sense of obligation when she saved his life in battle?

Kaikeyi to the rescue

Kaikeyi once joined Dashratha on his war chariot when the Devas summoned him to join them in their fight with the Asuras. In the middle of this battle, the axle of the chariot broke. The chariot would have surely toppled but for Kaikeyi's timely intervention. She leaned over the side of the chariot and used her arm to replace the broken axle. Dashratha was so grateful to Kaikeyi that he offered her two boons, anything she wished. Kaikeyi told her husband that she would ask for these boons at an appropriate time.

Dashratha feels so indebted by Kaikeyi's actions that he lavishes her with affection by offering to give her whatever she desires. She desires nothing, she clarifies, content to save her husband's life. 'But when you do, I will grant it to you. Not one, but two wishes,' says Dashratha, indulgently. The *Ramayana* holds this lack of royal discipline as the root cause of turmoil.

Years later, after Manthara, the maid, stokes the flames of insecurity and ambition, Kaikeyi finally asks for her boons.

Manthara's tirade

Kaikeyi's maid, Manthara, was furious when she learnt that Ram was to be crowned king, and that too when Bharata was away at his maternal uncle's home. Had Kaikeyi's father not given Kaikeyi's hand in marriage only after Dashratha assured him that her son would follow him to the throne? Incensed, she strode into Kaikeyi's chambers only to find the queen celebrating the news of Ram's coronation. 'He is like my own son,' Kaikeyi said. Manthara beat her chest, banged her head against the wall and spat out all the venom in her heart. At the end of her tirade, Kaikeyi was convinced that her husband had wronged her. When her husband would depart to the forest, she, the palace favourite, and her son would be at the mercies of Ram and his mother. Having finally made her mistress see her way, Manthara advised Kaikeyi on how she could remedy the situation.

Manthara symbolizes the dark side of kama or desire and how it breeds unhappiness, suspicion and anxiety. She casts aspersions on Dashratha's integrity: why was the coronation taking place while Bharata was away at his maternal uncle's house? Given this, Kaikeyi's first boon, that Bharata should be made king in place of Ram, seems fair, even appropriate. It ensures that Dashratha does not go back on his promise to Kaikeyi's father.

But why did Kaikeyi have to ask for the second boon, insisting that Ram go to the forest? The simplest answer given is that Kaikeyi did not want any rivals to the throne around when her son was crowned king. But then why was the exile given for a finite period of time? Why only fourteen years? Why not forever?

The purpose is revealed in Ramopakhyan, the tale of Ram narrated by Rishi Markandeya to the Pandavas in the epic *Mahabharata*.

Gandharvi Manthara

Brahma, father of all living creatures, directed a Gandharvi to descend on earth as Manthara and poison the mind of Kaikeyi so that Ram would be forced to leave Ayodhya and live in the forest for fourteen years where he could rid the world of Rakshasas and their king, Ravana, thus making the world a safer place.

A new dimension is thus revealed: karma or destiny. Ram is no mere prince; he is God destined to walk the earth to rid the forest of demons. Kaikeyi's ambition and Dashratha's integrity were merely tools to make this happen. With this story, Ram's exile is no longer a tragedy but a necessity.

Thus the birth of Ram is not just desired by Dashratha, it is also pre-destined. Vishnu, who is God, descends on earth with the intention of killing Ravana. Dashratha's yagna gives him a timely conduit to descend on earth. Vishnu is accompanied by his serpent, Adi-Sesha, who is born as Lakshman, his discus who is born as Bharata and his conch-shell who is born as Shatrughna. Other gods join him too, later in the epic, as he prepares to fight Ravana. Brahma descends as the bear Jambavan and Shiva descends as Hanuman. But mortal eyes, unaware of divinity's grand plan, weep on learning of Ram's fate.

People of Ayodhya

News that Ram was not going to be king and that he was instead ordered to spend fourteen years in the forest as a hermit was met with disbelief in Ayodhya. The people gathered around the palace to find out if this was true. They let out a wail when they saw the obedient young prince stepping out with his wife and brother dressed in clothes of bark. Behind him was the king clearly distraught. The king's charioteer, companion and chief advisor, Sumantra, brought out the royal chariot. 'Ride on this till the city gates at least,' he said. Ram agreed if only to make his way through the crowds of people who were blocking the streets. 'Don't go. Don't go,' they cried. They screamed and shouted and cursed Kaikeyi. But they all calmed down when they saw Ram's face and realized he did not appreciate such a display of rage. 'If Ram will not be our king, we will not stay in Ayodhya,' said the people. When Ram alighted from the chariot and started walking towards the forest, all the people of Ayodhya followed him. Ram realized that they would not leave his side. So at night, when everyone was asleep, he slipped away. Sumantra tried to follow him but Ram respectfully requested Sumantra to return to Ayodhya and serve his father who needed him more. He also begged Sumantra to tell his people to treat all his mothers, Kaikeyi included, with love and respect. With a heavy heart, Sumantra finally turned around, overwhelmed by the young prince's magnanimity.

As he watched Ram go, a heartbroken Dashratha wondered why he had to suffer so. At this, his guru, Vasishtha, reminded him of an event which took place long ago.

Shravana-kumar

During a hunt, Dashratha heard a sound which he assumed was made by a deer drinking water. Without bothering to check, Dashratha shot an arrow in the direction of the sound and discovered, to his horror, that he had struck a boy who was collecting water from the pond. The boy, Shravana, was the only child and caregiver of his old blind parents. When the old couple learnt of their son's fate, they cursed Dashratha that he, like them, would lose his son and die of the heartache that would follow.

Ram's exile then becomes just the fulfilment of the curse of Shravana's parents — an event that was supposed to happen.

In Hindu mythology, curses and boons are narrative tools to explain the concept of karma. The law of karma states that one's action has a reaction that one is obliged to experience if not in this life then in the next. Boons represent punya, a good action that results in a good reaction while curses represent paap, a bad action that results in a bad reaction. By saving her husband's life, Kaikeyi does a punya for which she gets two boons while by killing Shravana, Dashratha does paap for which he pays dearly. Paap and punya determine all events in this ever-changing world known as samsara. Nothing in samsara is spontaneous. Everything is the result of something else. All events are bound to happen.

The *Ramayana* reflects how people respond to such pre-destined events of life. Sometimes, one must surrender to fate just as Dashratha did when Ram left for the forest. But at other times, one must fight back like Dashratha did when he was unable to father a child after the birth of Shanta. Not only did he marry two more women, he also performed a destiny-subverting ritual.

Destiny and desire, karma and kama, are the two forces that propel the world. Destiny is a reaction, an obligation that follows an action. Desire is an aspiration that forces the world to transform in a particular way. Destiny creates fate. Desire is based on free will. We have the freedom to accept life as it is or to make it the way we want it to be. That is what makes us Manavas or humans.

Kaikeyi had the option of not saving her husband's life. She did it nevertheless. Dashratha had the option of not giving her two boons. He did it nevertheless. Kaikeyi had the option of never asking for those boons. She did it nevertheless. Dashratha had the option of turning down her boons. He, however, chose to keep his word. That is why Ram was exiled. At the same time, Ram's exile was destined. Having killed Shravana, Dashratha's heart had to be broken. And Vishnu had to, as Ram, kill Ravana and this could only happen if he left Ayodhya. Thus the exile of Ram, like all things in this world, is both destined and desired.

Desire and destiny make life unpredictable and uncertain. When things change constantly, people feel insecure. When nothing is permanent, there is frustration and sorrow. In despair and disgust, humans withdraw from society and become hermits, trying to break free and understand the point of it all. But there is another choice, another way to live, states the *Ramayana*. It is the code of conduct known as dharma.

The word 'dharma' is derived from the root 'dhr' which means 'to uphold or stabilize or make secure'. It is a manmade construct that creates civilization. Civilization is essentially a shelter from the world's impermanent and unpredictable nature. It is created when humans, unlike animals, look beyond self-preservation and self-propagation. It is created when the beneficiary of human action is not just the self, but others around us. One way of creating civilization is to do one's duty, not what one wants for oneself but what one is expected to do for the larger good.

When Dashratha agrees to fulfil Kaikeyi's wishes, it is certainly not for his own happiness. His reason is most eloquently expressed by Goswami Tulsidas in his celebrated sixteenth century work, the *Ram-charit-manas*:

> *Raghukula riti sada chali aai, prana jahu,*
> *baru bachanu na jaaee*

> So has been the way of my ancestors: give
> up your life but never your word

In a world where people do what they want, keeping promises only when it suits them, there are no guarantees, hence no sense of security, and in other words, no civilization. As king, it is Dashratha's duty to establish civilization. He is therefore expected to keep his word, even if it means sending his faultless son into exile. Dashratha makes this difficult choice.

Ram leaves Ayodhya, not because it is his destiny and not because it is his desire, but because it is his duty. He must do what sons are supposed to do, especially since he is the member of the royal family, an example to his subjects.

By choosing dharma, Dashratha and his son conquer the vagaries of life created by karma and kama. They create a society where people are liberated from feeling helpless before fate, and from being overwhelmed by free will. The desire to withdraw from the world and become hermits wanes. Under the responsible mantle of the king and his son, hermits become householders, unafraid to face this world of no guarantees.

3

Vishwamitra's Student

O Chief of Raghus!
No one else but you bestows me with affection
None but you protects me
O Lord of the Universe!
Most exalted among men!
Who else but you
Would have donated Lanka to Vibhishana
To the delight of Indra and others?
Who else but you
Would have followed Vishwamitra from Ayodhya
And protected his sacrifice from desecration
By Maricha and others?
Who else but you
Could have killed the mighty Vali
With a single arrow
And crowned Sugriva, the king of Kishkindha?
Please hold the hand of innocent Tyagaraja
Enable him to cross
This ocean of worldly problems

—From the songs of the eighteenth-century Tamil
poet-singer Tyagaraja

Facing worldly reality

Ram is educated by two Rishis: first Vasishtha and then Vishwamitra. Rishis are tapasvins, ascetics imbued with the power of tapa, which is heat generated through celibacy and other forms of sensory withdrawal. Tapa grants them the magical power known as siddhi.

Vasishtha is born a Rishi, created by Brahma himself, and is one of the seven primal custodians of Vedic wisdom. Vishwamitra, by contrast, is born a warrior who becomes a Rishi later in life by performing tapasya. Vishwamitra's approach to life is radically different from that of Vasishtha, so different in fact, that the Puranas portray the two Rishis as rivals.

It is Vishwamitra's arrival that marks the end of Ram's childhood and the beginning of his journey as a man.

Vishwamitra was born Kaushik, a prince, just like Ram. He once tried to forcibly lay hands on Vasishtha's magical cow, Nandini, which could fulfil any wish. This cow was a gift from the gods and Vasishtha protected the cow using his siddhi. Kaushik's weapons and army were no match for Vasishtha's spiritual powers. Humbled by the confrontation, Kaushik decided to become a Rishi himself by performing tapasya. Renouncing wife and children and kingdom, he went to the forest. Fearing that Kaushik would misuse the tapa that he would gather, Indra, king of the Devas, sent the nymph Menaka to seduce him. She succeeded but Kaushik refused to give up. Resuming his austerities, he once again controlled his senses and was able to discipline his mind, overpowering all temptations. Thus did he become a Rishi. It was then that he took the name of Vishwamitra meaning 'friend of the world'.

Indra, though the king of the Devas and god of the sky, is constantly shown as being very insecure. His abode, Swarg, the Hindu paradise, has the tree called Kalpataru, the cow called Kamadhenu and the gem called Chintamani. This tree, cow and gem fulfil all desires and manifest every dream. So in Indra's paradise there is no hunger, no lack of anything. Indra even has amrit, the nectar of immortality. He thus suffers no disease and does not have to fear death. And yet, Indra is eternally anxious, terrified of losing all that he has. Thus the *Ramayana* concludes that material fulfilment does not grant contentment. That is why Vasishtha refuses to give his holy cow to Kaushik; he would rather share his wisdom that will help man outgrow the desire to possess any wish-fulfilling cow.

But Kaushik does not believe this. He values material things. His transformation into Vishwamitra is based on his firm belief that siddhis attained through tapa can and should be used to help humanity cope with material discontentment, and this difference in approach is clear in the way he instructs Ram.

As Dashratha's guru, it is Vasishtha's duty to educate Ram. The education is completed with a dialogue that is today considered the most sophisticated document on yoga known as Yoga Vasishtha. In it, Vasishtha introduces Ram to the nature of the world and advises him on what his relationship should be with the world. The dialogue reveals how to engage with the world without being attached to it.

Yoga Vasishtha

After completing his education under Vasishtha, Ram and his brothers went on a long pilgrimage. On their return, Dashratha noticed that Ram had lost all interest in things worldly. Since nothing is permanent, Ram wondered what was the purpose of life. When Dashratha informed Vasishtha of this, the guru said, 'Now he is ready to receive the instruction on yoga.' Vasishtha then taught Ram the doctrine of the soul and the body. Ram learnt how the body encloses the mind that senses the world and responds to it. He learnt how the immortal soul witnesses the sensations and responses of the mortal flesh. He was able to appreciate the purpose of an ever-changing world as a medium to realize the never-changing soul.

Ram's education under Vasishtha is barely complete when Vishwamitra storms into Dashratha's court and demands Ram's services. It seems as if Vishwamitra feels Ram's education under Vasishtha is too theoretical and quite incomplete. Ram needs to see the world and gain practical experience. Ram must know the trials and tribulations of the material world that he has been sheltered from in his father's palace and his guru's hermitage. In other words, Vishwamitra comes to Dashratha's palace determined to initiate Ram into adulthood.

Vishwamitra's yagna

Vishwamitra said he was planning to perform a yagna in the forest and he needed the young prince

Ram to protect the sacrificial precinct from attacks by Rakshasas. At first, Dashratha hesitated; he was willing to send his entire army to the forest to guard the yagna, but not Ram. 'He is too young to fight the demons on his own,' said the king. Vishwamitra was adamant and refused to settle for anyone but Ram. At this point, Vasishtha intervened. He advised the king to let Ram go with Vishwamitra for it was Ram's duty as prince to serve and protect sages. Besides Vishwamitra would ensure Ram came to no harm. If pleased, the great Vishwamitra would even share with Ram the secret knowledge of celestial weapons. Finally, rather reluctantly, Dashratha let Ram go. Lakshman, as usual, followed Ram.

Ram is wrenched out of his zone of comfort when he sets out with Vishwamitra. The cutting of the umbilical cord begins with the horrific act of killing a woman.

Tadaka

The forest where Vishwamitra wanted to perform his yagna was the lair of a Rakshasa woman called Tadaka. Tadaka was once a Yaksha woman, daughter of Suketu, wife of Sunda. She attacked Rishi Agastya when the latter killed her husband following a confrontation in the forest. Seeing her rush towards him like a monster, Agastya cursed her to become a Rakshasa. Since then, Tadaka had terrorized all the Rishis in the forest. She was determined to stop Vishwamitra's yagna. When she appeared before Ram, Vishwamitra ordered Ram to kill her. Ram hesitated; Tadaka was a woman after all. Vishwamitra argued that man or woman, a creature that harms the innocent must be killed for the larger good. Accordingly, Ram raised his bow and shot the Rakshasa woman dead.

This story introduces us to two classes of beings: Yakshas and Rakshasas. These, along with another class of beings known as Gandharvas, repeatedly find mention in the epic. Typically, Rishis encounter them as they wander through the forest in their spiritual quest. The interaction is sometimes friendly with the Rishi either being accepted as guru or as a son-in-law. But often it is violent resulting in curses being hurled and pitched battles being fought. It seems most likely that these 'magical creatures' of the forest were those who did not follow the Vedic way of life based on the code of dharma. The relatively friendly tribes were called Yakshas or Gandharvas while the hostile ones were

Devdutt Pattanaik

deemed Rakshasas, a term which eventually became synonymous with demons.

Being a Rakshasa is reason enough for Tadaka to be killed by Ram. But Tadaka is a woman, hence Ram, a student of Vasishtha, hesitates. Women create life within their bodies. To kill a woman is to kill life. It is the worst crime in the Vedic world. Vishwamitra disagrees: gender does not matter, behaviour does. Tadaka must be killed because she is violently hostile to the way of dharma, an act that cannot be excused on account of her womanhood. And so Ram raises his bow and strikes her dead. For this, Ram is rewarded with mantras that can transform his arrows into deadly missiles.

Magical weapons of Vishwamitra

Pleased with Ram's obedience, Vishwamitra gave Ram many shastras and astras, weapons and missiles. He taught Ram potent chants by which he could imbue the tips of his arrows with the power of fire and rain and wind. These were magical weapons with which he could fight alongside the gods and defeat any demon.

Vishwamitra has clearly mastered the occult powers he once watched Vasishtha use against his army. And he shares this with a prince so that the prince can use it to make the world a happier and safer place.

Maricha and Subahu

As Vishwamitra's yagna progressed, many Rakshasas attacked the sacrificial precinct hurling rocks and bones to stop the ritual. But they were all driven back or killed by Ram and Lakshman who kept a constant vigil around the site for six days and six nights. On the last day, the Rakshasa hordes, led by Maricha and Subahu, tried to pour blood in the fire altar. Ram released two arrows. With one, he pushed Maricha far away in the southern direction. With the other, he killed Subahu. Then both brothers dispatched the remaining demons with a rain of missiles. Thus under the protection of Ram and Lakshman, Vishwamitra was able to complete his yagna.

In the *Ramayana*, Rakshasas represent a way of life where all behaviour is instinctual and self-indulgent, governed by fear and insecurity. Rishis represent the opposite way of life, where all instincts, be they sexual or violent, are regulated for the benefit of the world. Ram's conquest of the Rakshasas is thus the symbolic

Devdutt Pattanaik

subjugation of man's primal instincts by more evolved values based on sharing and caring.

Vishwamitra makes Ram the defender of dharma, the way of life championed by Rishis—a way of life based on rules not impulse, where sex is allowed only for self-propagation, that is, within marriage for children and where violence is allowed only for self-preservation, for food and in defence.

In the world defined by Rishis, husbands and wives are expected to be absolutely faithful to each other. But sometimes, desire overpowers the mind and rules are forgotten. Lines are transgressed. This happens to Ahalya who is horribly punished for it by her husband.

Ahalya

Gautam, a Rishi, once returned home to find his wife, Ahalya, in the arms of Indra, king of the Devas. Furious, he castrated Indra and cursed his wife to turn into stone. On Vishwamitra's instruction, Ram placed his foot on the stone that was Ahalya. Instantly, Ahalya was cleansed of her misdeed and resumed her human form.

When Indra touches Ahalya, she is polluted, when Gautam touches her, she is punished, but when Ram touches Ahalya, she is liberated. Ram does not desire Ahalya like Indra. Ram does not berate Ahalya like Gautam. Guided by Vishwamitra, he forgives her lapse for he recognizes and makes room for human frailty, something that Vasishtha perhaps would not allow.

Vishwamitra believes that Ram's experience with Tadaka and Ahalya has initiated him into adulthood, made him see the contextual nature of things. While one woman deserved death in one set of circumstances, another deserved compassion in another set of circumstances. With this understanding of the relative nature of things, Vishwamitra believes, Ram is ready to become a householder. He takes the prince to Mithila, capital of Videha.

Breaking the bow

Janaka, king of Mithila, invited Ram to string the mighty bow of Shiva that was in his custody. If he succeeded, he could marry his daughter, Sita. Ram learnt that many had tried before and failed. The bow was so heavy that many gods and demons had been unable even to lift it, let alone string it. Ram decided to try his luck. To everyone's surprise, the young Ram was not only able to raise the bow, he was even able to bend it. He bent it so hard that the shaft of the bow broke. Impressed by the boy's strength, Janaka gave Sita's hand in marriage to Ram. Sita's younger sister, Urmila, and her cousins, Mandavi and Shutakirti, daughters of Janaka's younger brother, Kushadhvaja, were given as wives to Ram's younger brothers, Lakshman, Bharata and Shatrughna.

The marriage of Ram to Sita marks the end of Ram's education under Vishwamitra. The prince who left Ayodhya a boy returns as a man.

Vasishtha's Ram was a wise sage, well versed in the scriptures and in knowledge of the spirit. But Vishwamitra's Ram has experienced the world. He knows that in the real world, people, in fear and out of desire, will hurt and betray each other. A king has to resolve such situations, not with highhandedness, but with empathy and compassion.

But the Ram who returns to Ayodhya is also the one who broke Shiva's bow when he was asked to string it by Janaka. While everyone cheers this achievement, the significance of this detail is often overlooked.

If the bow is a symbol of poise and balance, by breaking it, did not Ram display a moment of excessiveness? The bow belongs to Shiva, the supreme ascetic, the embodiment of detachment. By breaking it, has Ram displayed, under Vishwamitra's influence perhaps, an excess of passion? Perhaps that is why Ram is not yet ready to be king. Perhaps that is why, even though Dashratha is eager to pass on the crown, it is necessary for Ram to evolve further. That is why, perhaps, Vasishtha does not intervene when the eldest son of Dashratha is forced to live in the forest as a hermit for fourteen years. That is where Ram shall tame his excessive passions, learn the limitations of all things material, observe the folly of desire and return ready to be a great king.

4

Sita's Husband

I salute that divinity called Ram
Who lightened the load of the earth
Who lead his people to satisfaction
Who is the sun who puts an end to darkness

—From *Raghotham Ashtakam* that praises Ram,
scion of the Raghu clan, in eight Sanskrit verses

Value of chastity

Sita is a special child. She has no father or mother. She is ayonija, one who is not conceived in a womb. She was named Sita because she was found in a furrow at the end of a plough.

Birth of Sita

As part of a farming festival, Janaka, king of Videha, was ploughing a field using a hoe of gold. To his astonishment, he ploughed a girl child out of the earth. This was the gift of the earth goddess to the childless Janaka. Janaka named her Sita and adopted her as his daughter. She therefore became renowned as Maithili, princess of Mithila, as Vaidehi, princess of Videha, and as Janaki, daughter of Janaka.

Ram comes seeking Sita's hand in marriage after killing a woman called Tadaka and rescuing another woman called Ahalya. Tadaka is a wild and violent Rakshasa woman, Ahalya is an unfaithful wife. Sita by contrast is domestic and chaste. Thus, the three women represent three aspects of womanhood. Tadaka subscribes to no rules, Ahalya breaks a rule while Sita follows all rules.

All three women also symbolize three forms of the earth. That Sita represents farmed land is made quite explicit through the tale of her birth where she emerges as the earth is being ploughed. Ahalya's association with the earth is more subtle. Hala means plough. Ahalya therefore means land that is unfit to be ploughed. If Sita, the domestic wife represents farming land then Ahalya, the unfaithful wife, can be understood as a representation of land not fit for ploughing and the wild Tadaka symbolizes wild land which has not been domesticated. Through these implicit associations of women with the various forms of earth (cultivated, fallow and wild), the *Ramayana* reveals its subliminal messages.

Sita is domestic and chaste because Ram pays her attention. Ahalya is unfaithful because Gautam neglects her. Tadaka is wild because her husband is dead and she is attached to no single man. Thus the onus of maintaining a field falls squarely on a farmer. In his absence, anarchy reigns: the field becomes fallow, and then a forest. Civilization is best represented by a fertile, domesticated and fenced field. Man, the farmer, can create or destroy civilization by his attention or neglect.

At a symbolic level, the forest and field are metaphors for the mind. The forest is the untamed mind. The field is the domesticated mind. The consciousness is the farmer. If one is conscious like Ram, faithful and attentive, the mind will be like Sita. When one is conscious like Gautam, ignoring the mind, the mind will be seduced by temptation. In the absence of awareness, the mind will be wild with no direction.

Shiva's bow

Janaka, king of Videha, was the custodian of a bow that belonged to Shiva. It was a heavy bow. At least a dozen servants were required to pick it up and clean it. Sita, however, was able to pick it up with ease and play with it as if it were a toy. She would pretend it was a horse and ride it. When a sage called Parashuram noticed this, he realized Sita was no ordinary girl. He advised Janaka to give Sita's hand in marriage only to a man who was worthy of her, one who had the power to at least string the mighty bow that she used for play.

Sita's power that is evident in this story needs to be contained and directed towards home building and child rearing. At birth, it is implied, all women are forests, raw and untamed, belonging to no one in particular. It is the responsibility of fathers, brothers, husbands and sons to transform women into fields — fencing them, controlling their fertility, deciding which seed should germinate in their soil.

The idea that Vedic India saw women only as daughters, sisters, wives and mothers reeks of patriarchy. Patriarchy, however, assumes the curtailment of a woman's freedom, not a man's. But in Vedic India, everyone's freedom was curtailed. Duty formed the cornerstone of Vedic civilization. All duties were determined at the moment of birth. Just as a woman's fate was fettered to her womanhood, a man's fate was fettered to his manhood. A male child was expected to follow his father's vocation whether he liked it or not. This was varna-dharma. Ram had no choice but to be a warrior like his father. Even if he wished it, he would not have been allowed to be a musician or a trader. The only other option available to him was to renounce

Devdutt Pattanaik

society altogether and be a hermit. Society even decided at what age a man should marry and at what age he should retire. This was ashrama-dharma.

Varna-ashrama-dharma established by Manu, the first king of mankind, curtailed choices and restrained freedom, because desire was seen as the primary threat to order. In this system, everyone had duties but no one had any rights. Rights were seen as self-indulgent. As a member of society, men and women were supposed to live for others.

Sita follows Ram

When news reached Sita that Ram had been asked by his father to live in the forest for fourteen years, she decides to follow him. 'But life there will be terrible,' said Ram, determined to dissuade her. 'Wild animals, hostile tribes, demons, whimsical weather, no place to stay, no guarantee of food. No, stay back in the palace. Take care of my old parents.' To this Sita replied, 'Ever since I was a child, oracles have predicted that I will spend much of my life in the forest. I have been looking forward to going to the forest. It has never terrified me. I shall withstand the weather and the hunger. I shall face the wild animals and the hostile tribes. I shall follow you quietly. You will not find me a burden. Quietly I shall endure the treacherous wilderness and give you not a moment to complain.' Ram, however, insisted that Sita stay back. 'What are you afraid of? I cannot believe that my father gave me such a weak man as a husband, ' she berated him. 'Can't you see: with you by my side, the most terrifying of forests shall be better than the most comfortable of palaces? Without you, I would rather die,' saying this, Sita wept. Ram finally agreed to let Sita accompany him.

Sita knows her place in the world. It is to be her husband's shadow. So she follows him into the forest. If Ram had had his way, she would have stayed back in the palace. But Ram is her husband, not her master. As his wife, she has duties towards him but he has no rights over her.

Like Ram, Sita prepares to wear clothes of bark when it is time to leave for the forest. But the palace women stop her from removing her bridal finery.

In Vedic times, at the time of marriage, a girl was bedecked with sixteen symbols that transformed her from a woman into a wife. These symbols included (the list varies in different texts): parting the hair; smearing

Devdutt Pattanaik

the parting of the hair with vermilion powder; knotting the hair into a bun; decorating the hair with strings of flowers; sandal paste and perfumes over the body; a red sari; earrings for the ears; kohl around the eyes; nose ring for the nose; necklaces and garlands around the neck, especially the mangalsutra or the string of marriage; bangles, bracelets and armlets for the arms, rings for the hands; anklets with tiny bells for the legs, toe rings for the feet; alta or red dye for the palms and the soles; chewing betel nut wrapped in betel leaves.

Sita is not allowed to remove any of these symbols as she remains Ram's wife even in the forest. These symbols distinguish her from an unmarried girl and a widow. Only when the husband dies were wives asked to remove these sixteen symbols. To do so before was to bring bad luck to the husband's household.

In the forest, Ram and Sita pay a visit to the hermitage of sage Atri where his wife, Anasuya, gifts Sita with a sari that will never tear or get soiled. Thus her marital status is not just reinforced but celebrated.

In temples where a goddess is enshrined, the primary offering to the deity is either fabric like a sari or a blouse piece, or jewellery like nose rings and bangles, or cosmetics like kajal or alta. Implicit in this ritual offering is the desire that the goddess become a bride and mother. Without these offerings, the goddess is naked. Unclothed, she is the wild and violent Kali, much like Tadaka. Clothed, she becomes Gauri, the demure and domestic one, much like Sita. There is the constant fear that the goddess may return to her unbound primal state, that the field may become a forest. Perhaps that is why Ram does not want Sita to go to the forest. Perhaps that is why the palace does not want Sita to shed her bridal finery.

In the forest, Sita watches her husband kill demons and make the forest a safer place for sages. She feels that his violence is at times excessive and unprovoked. Ram does not think so. This conversation between the field and the farmer draws attention to the fact that a good king is supposed to know how much domestication of the forest is necessary for human needs and how much is too much.

Sages in the forest

After crossing the Ganga and Yamuna and staying for a while in Chitrakut on the advice of Rishi Bharadwaj, Ram and Sita along with Lakshman decided to move south exploring the dense wilderness known as Dandaka. There they encountered demons like Viradha and sages like

Shrabhanga. They killed the demons so that the forest was safer for sages. So passed thirteen years. In the final year of exile, they met Rishi Agastya, who gave Ram many weapons and thanked him for making the forest a safer place by eliminating numerous demons. Directed by the sage, they went to the woods known as Panchavati.

The field is constantly under threat of being overwhelmed by the forest. Thus, while in the forest, as Sita walks behind Ram, she does attract the roving eye of men, despite wearing all the symbols indicating she is someone else's wife.

Crow's eye

A crow kept chasing and pecking Sita. She endured the harassment silently. When Ram saw what the crow was doing, he was so incensed that he picked up a blade of grass, chanted a mantra and hurled it at the crow. The crow turned out to be none other than Jayanta, Indra's son, who harassed Sita in order to test if Ram was really God. He ran across the three worlds to escape Ram's grass missile. Finally, he begged Ram to forgive him for doubting his divinity. Sita intervened too. And so Ram said the missile would not kill the crow. It would only pierce one of its eyes. Since then crows are supposed to have only one eye.

Jayanta is Indra's son, the same Indra who seduced Ahalya. This is no coincidence. Indra is renowned in mythology as a god who seeks to seduce women unaccompanied by men. Finding a woman dressed in bridal finery accompanied by hermits, who are supposed to be celibate, Indra's son clearly assumes Sita is unattached and available. He pecks her and even scratches her breasts ostensibly for food. But Ram is not amused. He knows what the vile creature seeks and he punishes him without mercy. Thus the farmer protects the field.

The story is narrated by Sita to Hanuman when he locates her in Lanka. This story, she tells him, is a secret known only to her and her husband. Clearly, the two do not want this to be public knowledge. It stains their royal reputation and highlights the worst fear people have about the forest—beyond the frontiers of civilization women are exposed to a realm where the laws of marriage have no hold, and are hence liable to break free from the shackles of dharma.

As a hermit, Ram has to stay celibate. In the forest, he witnesses the freedom of nature, birds and beasts

Devdutt Pattanaik

responding to instinct and mating in public. But bound by his word, forced to be a hermit for fourteen years, he must restrain himself from being intimate with his young wife. His commitment to his word is thus tested to the limits. Ram's celibacy is never explicitly stated in the epic but is alluded to by the fact that despite being in the forest for fourteen years, Sita never gets pregnant. Across India, there are many spots associated with Ram and Sita. Typically, there are separate ponds where Ram and Sita performed their ablutions, suggesting the distance they maintained between them.

Like Ram, Lakshman too follows the path of the hermit. Beside him is his beautiful sister-in-law who any man would desire. But he does not even look at her. Thus he keeps his natural instincts under check. The following story comes from Ekanath's *Bhavarth Ramayana* written in Marathi.

Clothes of Sita

Once while Ram was away foraging for food in the forest, Sita and Lakshman were busy setting up a shelter using branches and leaves of a tree. Having done so Sita fell to the ground exhausted and decided to take a nap. Lakshman sat with his back to Sita while she slept. Suddenly the wind blew and Sita's robes got disarrayed and her body was exposed. Ram returned and saw this and asked Lakshman, 'She lies there almost unclothed. What a beautiful woman she is! Who can restrain their passions at the sight of one such as her?' To this Lakshman replied, 'He whose father is Dashratha and whose mother is Sumitra and whose brother is Ram is the one who can restrain his passion at a sight that he has never seen but has only heard you describe.' Ram was touched by his brother's purity of character.

This story highlights what distinguishes human society from the jungle. In the jungle, sex is instinctual but in the human world it is governed by both emotions and intellect. In the jungle, all males are attracted to the female in season but only the most powerful or most beautiful or most skilled male is allowed to mate with her. In some species, the selection is done by the female. In others, the males fight amongst themselves and the winner alone pursues the female. But in human society, law, not power, binds man to woman. Every man has a spouse and the two are expected to be faithful to each other. In human society, man even has the option of conquering his sexual urge, even when a woman is available, something that is not seen in the natural world.

Sita is in a peculiar situation: she is a wife but her husband does not touch her because he is forced to be a hermit. She is constantly in the company of another man, Lakshman, who is not her husband. Their close proximity can breed attraction but both Sita and Lakshman overpower these natural instincts by their adherence to dharma. Thus, Ram, Lakshman and Sita, by being chaste, embody civilized conduct. They may have left Ayodhya but Ayodhya has not left them. By upholding dharma, they do not let the forest make animals of them.

Surpanakha, however, does not adhere to the code of civilization. She is therefore deemed a Rakshasa. Like Tadaka, she is the wilderness. She follows her desire.

Surpanakha

One day, a Rakshasa woman called Surpanakha saw Ram and was smitten by his beauty. She approached him and made her intention very clear. 'I am married,' said Ram, 'But my brother there is alone. Go to him.' Surpanakha went to Lakshman but even he turned her down. 'I left my wife behind so that I can serve my brother and his wife all the time. I have no time for you. I am my brother's servant. It is better you were a king's second wife than a servant's first.' Surpanakha did not take this rejection kindly. She was determined to have Ram and she surmised that if she could get Sita out of the way, Ram would change his mind. So she rushed towards Sita, displaying her true monstrous form, baring her fangs and claws. Sita screamed and Lakshman rushed to her rescue. He pulled the Rakshasa woman back and with his arrowhead cut her nose and ears. A mutilated Surpanakha screamed in agony and called out to Khar and Dushan who rushed to her rescue and attacked Ram and Lakshman. The two brothers, however, were able to drive the demons away with ease.

Surpanakha is behaving as a creature of the forest would behave. She wants Ram and she expresses her desire freely, without embarrassment. But Ram is not of the forest. He clings to dharma and rejects the proposal. Surpanakha responds as forest creatures would, with force. Lakshman then reacts as a city dweller would — he strikes her with the intention of taming her.

Lakshman does not kill Surpanakha as Ram had killed Tadaka. Sita is responsible for this restraint. During their stay in the forest, Sita watches Ram and Lakshman constantly fight and kill Rakshasas. She expresses her displeasure. She feels that weapons should be used with discretion — to domesticate rather than destroy the wild. And so while under Vishwamitra's guidance, Ram had killed Tadaka, under Sita's influence Surpanakha is spared.

But Surpanakha is brutally mutilated — her nose, her ears and her breasts are sliced off. This disfiguration is aimed at curtailing her aggressive sexuality. The viciousness of the punishment sparks a conflagration that both Ram and Lakshman cannot escape. For such is the law of karma.

Rather than domesticating Surpanakha, Lakshman ends up angering her. Scorned and abused by the brothers, Surpanakha goes to her brother and demands vengeance.

Surpanakha's brother

Surpanakha was the sister of Ravana, king of the Rakshasas. Ravana had accidentally killed Surpanakha's husband and to make amends, he had told his sister that she had the freedom to go to any man she pleased to satisfy her carnal desires. And so Surpanakha roamed the forests along with her companions, Khar and Dushan, enjoying the company of any man who caught her eye. But one day, Surpanakha returned, her face and body horribly mutilated by two hermits, Ram and Lakshman, who were residing in the woods of Panchavati. She told her brother all that happened. 'By hurting me, they have insulted you. Punish them. Humiliate them. Make that wife of his, to whom he is so faithful, your concubine.' Ravana comforted his sister. His physicians took care of her while he made plans to teach the man who hurt his sister a lesson he would never forget.

As Ravana abducts Sita and takes her to Lanka on his flying chariot, she starts shedding her bridal finery that she hopes will serve as a trail for her husband to follow so that he can find and rescue her. The removal of jewellery is also symbolic. It is the removal of the clothes of the goddess. Gauri, the domesticated goddess of fields, is under threat of becoming Kali, the wild goddess of the forest. It forebodes the end of dharma, of civilization. In fact, when Hanuman finally finds Sita, she gives him a hairpin, the last of her jewellery. The giving of a hairpin is significant. Traditionally, in India, tied hair represents rules and restraint while untied hair represents lawlessness and freedom. It was inauspicious for a married woman to be seen in public with unbound hair. Loose hair meant loose morals. Only in the intimacy of her bedroom in the company of her husband was a woman allowed to unbind her hair. As soon as she stepped out of bed, the hair had to be tied. By sending her hairpin to Ram, Sita is giving a very powerful message: her wifely status is under threat. She represents the civilized world that Ram is supposed to protect. Ravana threatens her, hence all of civilization.

There are many stories to explain why Ravana did not force himself upon Sita. According to one tale, he was prevented from doing so on account of a curse.

Nalkuber

Ravana forced himself on Rambha, wife of his own nephew, Nalkuber. In fury Nalkuber cursed Ravana that if he ever abused any other woman this way his head would split into a thousand pieces.

Other stories, however, say that Sita was quite capable of protecting herself using the power of her chastity.

Ravana's threats

Ravana kept Sita prisoner in a garden. There she was given many gifts to lure her into his bed. But she refused them all. He threatened to kill her but she refused to submit to him. She placed a blade of grass between herself and Ravana and said that she had been a chaste wife all her life and if he dared take her by force the power of her chastity would kill him instantly. Ravana therefore kept away from her and used all methods to make Sita come to him willingly. Even his wives and her prison guards tried to tell her the benefits of being Ravana's wife and the perils of refusing him. But Sita refused to budge. None but Ram would rule her heart.

While Ravana had tricked Sita to physically cross Lakshman's line, she refused to cross the line intellectually and emotionally. The *Ramayana* repeatedly states how many women abandoned their husbands and went to Ravana's bed lured by his beauty and power. The women who guard Sita in Ravana's orchard keep describing his riches and his sexual prowess. But Sita refuses to succumb to these temptations.

Ram's severed head

Once Ravana came to Sita carrying the severed head of Ram. 'Look, I have killed Ram. Now you are bound to him no more. You can be my queen with no obligations to anyone.' Sita smiled and said, 'I am not fooled by your magical illusions. Had Ram really been killed, I would have died that very instant. I love him so deeply that our souls are entwined. His death will surely be the end of me. So go away and keep your lies to yourself.'

At another time Ravana takes her on his flying chariot over the battlefield and shows her the dead bodies of Ram and Lakshman. Sita wonders if this is true until she is told by the other Rakshasa women, who come to admire her for her uprightness, that Ravana's flying chariot would lose its power of flight if a widow stepped on it. That it was able to fly with Sita on it indicated that Sita was no widow, that the dead body of Ram shown by Ravana was actually an illusion created by him.

When Hanuman offers to carry Sita across the sea on his shoulders, Sita refuses the offer so that her husband does not lose the opportunity to regain his honour. She does this also because contact with another man, however chaste he may be, will dishonour her. Thus the *Ramayana* constantly and superlatively highlights both Sita's sexuality and her chastity.

Hindu mythology is full of tales of magical powers that women come to possess when they are chaste. In one folk narrative, Sita even uses the power of chastity to save Ram in battle. This story comes from the *Govind Ramayana* written by the tenth guru of the Sikhs, Guru Gobind Singh, in the seventeenth century.

The Naga mantra

Ravana's son, Indrajit, was a master of serpent magic. He struck both Ram and Lakshman with arrows imbued with the power of serpents. Within moments a deadly venom started spreading through their limbs. Indrajit rushed back to inform his father of his success. An ecstatic Ravana ordered that Sita be taken to the highest tower of Lanka and be shown her dying husband and brother-in-law. When Sita saw the two lying unconscious on the battlefield overwhelmed by snake venom and surrounded by helpless monkeys, she joined her palms and looked towards the earth and chanted a hymn in praise of Vasuki, the king of serpents. Such was the power of her chastity that Vasuki was forced to release an antidote that rendered powerless the poison running through the limbs of Ram and Lakshman.

Devdutt Pattanaik

In Hindu scriptures, great value is attached to Ravana's wife, Mandodari. Though wife of the demon-king, she does not behave like other Rakshasa women. She stands by her husband faithfully despite his unethical and immoral behaviour. This makes her a sati, just like Sita, the chaste wife, worthy of worship and adoration.

There are folk tales in which Ravana is protected from Ram's arrows by the power of the chastity of his wives. To kill Ravana, Hanuman flies over Lanka. His beautiful form enchants the wives of Ravana who for a moment experience desire for him. As a result, they lose the power of their chastity leaving Ravana unprotected and vulnerable.

Following Ravana's death, Sita is asked to prove her chastity publicly. It is one of the most humiliating moments in the *Ramayana*.

Trial by fire

After the death of Ravana, Sita expected Ram to personally liberate her from the orchard where she had been kept prisoner. Instead, Ram sent Vibhishana who requested her to bathe and prepare herself to go to Ram who waited for her on the battlefield. A dutiful Sita complied. To her surprise, Ram did not seem pleased to see her.

'I have done my duty. Restored my family honour. Killed the man who dared abduct my wife. Now you are free. Go to whoever you choose. You, who have stayed in Ravana's orchards for so long, are under no obligation to come to me,' Ram said. Sita was horrified to hear Ram's words. 'All these days I have thought of none but you,' she said. 'Not once have I submitted to Ravana. Let the world see how chaste I am. If I have been faithful to Ram then fire shall not harm me.' Lakshman was given the task of igniting a huge pyre. Sita calmly entered the fire. Everyone watched in wonderment as the flames did not scorch her skin or burn her hair. They all bowed, realizing that Sita was no ordinary woman. She was a goddess.

It is Sita's chastity that protects her from fire. When Hanuman burns Lanka, it is Sita's chastity that protects the orchard in which she is imprisoned. Ravana may have tried to violate her body but despite all his efforts he is unable to violate her heart or her soul. Lanka with all its riches is unable to corrupt Sita. She may be dragged to Lanka by her body but she refuses to abandon Ayodhya in her heart. Through her, the *Ramayana* reminds us that even a victim can be a winner if he or she refuses to surrender to the circumstance. People can conquer the land, people can conquer the body, but they can never conquer the mind. Thus, in the *Ramayana*, the field has a mind of its own. It is not a passive thing at the mercy of man or the elements. It has the power to be faithful to the farmer. That is what makes Sita an embodiment of the supremely cultivable land.

5

Lakshman's Brother

I repeatedly salute that Ramachandra
Who has a very playful body
Who is heroic in the battlefield
Who is the greatest hero in the universe
Who is the garland to the clan of Raghu
Who has a majestic voice
And who wins all arguments
I repeatedly salute that Ramachandra
Who appears frightening to the wicked person
Who appears submissive to the good person
Who is near to those who sing about him
Who shines greatly in his clan
Who is the song of the stars in the sky
And who is much beyond words

—From *Ramachandra Shatakam* that salutes Ram
in hundred Sanskrit verses

Loyalty or righteousness

Traditionally Indians are advised only to read the *Ramayana*, not the *Mahabharata*, inside the house because the *Ramayana* is the story of brothers doing everything in their power to keep the household united while the *Mahabharata* is the tale of a household divided over property. The *Ramayana* has three sets of brothers: those of Ram, those of Ravana and that of Sugriva.

Ram's brothers are devoted to him. It is said that soon after his birth, Lakshman kept crying until he was placed next to Ram. Since that day he was always beside Ram, accompanying him to protect Vishwamitra's yagna and following him into exile in the forest. Such was his devotion that he refused to take his wife along with him to the forest. He even refused to sleep for fourteen years so that he could serve his brother day and night. The following story is popular in the Ram-kavyas of Andhra Pradesh.

Urmila's sleep

Lakshman's wife wanted to follow her husband to the forest as Sita had followed Ram but he begged her to stay back. On the first night in the forest, Lakshman kept watch while Ram and Sita went to sleep. That is when Nidra, the goddess of sleep, approached him. He begged the goddess to leave him alone for fourteen years so that he could guard his brother and sister-in-law night and day. The goddess, impressed by his act of filial devotion, agreed. But the law of nature demanded that someone bear the burden of Lakshman's share of sleep. 'Go to my wife, Urmila, and inform her of the situation,' said Lakshman. Nidra went to Urmila. Urmila bowed her head and replied, 'Give me my husband's share of sleep for fourteen years so that he can stay awake all that time without any fatigue.' So it came to pass that Urmila slept for fourteen years, night and day while her husband stayed awake in the service of Ram and Sita.

Ram's other brother, Bharata, is equally devoted to him. He refuses to take advantage of his brother's misfortune. Instead he submits himself to the same suffering his brother has been subjected to.

Bharata's resolve

Bharata refused to take a kingdom obtained so deceitfully by his mother. He decided to go to the forest and bring his brother back. In the forest, from atop a tree, Lakshman saw Bharata followed by a vast army of men and women approaching Chitrakut, a hill where Ram and Sita had taken refuge. 'He plans to kill you,' said Lakshman. 'Let me kill him first.' Ram stopped his hot-headed brother from taking any rash steps. He was convinced that Bharata meant him no harm. And sure enough, when Bharata met Ram they hugged tearfully. Ram learnt of his father's death and was shattered. 'Come back. His kingdom needs you,' said Bharata. But Ram refused. His father's order that he stay as a hermit in the forest for fourteen years had to be fulfilled. Bharata then said, 'He did not order me to be king. The crown was simply secured for me by my mother's complicity. I reject it. Only Ram shall be king of Ayodhya. Until you return, I shall administer the kingdom as your regent. And during that time I shall not enjoy the comforts of royal life. I shall live as a hermit outside the city and suffer as you do. Let this be a lesson to my mother.' Bharata took Ram's sandals and carried them to Ayodhya and placed them on the throne. These would be the symbols of the king-in-exile.

By contrast, Ravana becomes king of Lanka by driving away his half-brother, Kuber, king of the Yakshas. The following story comes from Uttarkand, the final chapter of Valmiki's *Ramayana*.

Lord of Lanka

The sage Vishrava had two wives. From the first, he became the father of Kuber, who went on to become king of the Yakshas. From the second, Kaikesi, he became the father of Ravana, who went on to become king of the Rakshasas. Kuber built the golden city of Lanka on the island of Trikuta located in the middle of the southern sea. Jealous of his brother's prosperity, Ravana attacked the city of Lanka, drove his brother north and made himself king of Lanka.

The same behaviour is displayed by Sugriva's elder brother, Vali. The following story is based on the sixteenth-century Malayalam retelling of the *Ramayana* by Ezhuthachan.

Vali's quarrel

Riskha, king of Kishkindha, had asked his sons, Vali and Sugriva, to share the kingdom after him. Vali and his wife, Tara, lived happily with Sugriva and his wife, Ruma, for many years. Then one day a Rakshasa called Mayavi challenged Vali, who was renowned all over the world for his strength, to a duel. Vali overpowered Mayavi easily but then the demon gave Vali the slip and ran into a cave. 'I will follow him inside and kill him,' said Vali to Sugriva, 'But you stay here and guard the entrance of this cave and do not let him leave under any circumstances. If blood gushes out, remember it is I who have been killed but if milk gushes out remember it is not I but Mayavi who has been killed for milk not blood runs through Mayavi's veins.' Sugriva waited for a full year outside the cave but neither his brother nor the demon emerged from it. Inside the cave it was all dark and all he could hear were the sounds of fighting, the shouts of a demon and snarls of a monkey. At the end of the year there was silence. Blood started gushing out of the cave. Sugriva immediately assumed that Vali had been killed not realizing that before dying, Mayavi had cast a magic spell that made his blood appear red, not white. Sugriva called out to his brother but heard nothing. Sugriva was sure that Mayavi had killed his brother. Not wanting his brother's murderer to escape he rolled a huge boulder and blocked the entrance to the cave. Unfortunately, after the duel, Vali was too exhausted to shout and tell his brother of his victory. When he found the entrance of the cave blocked by a huge boulder, he suspected that Sugriva had done so with the intention of killing him. He kicked the boulder aside and returned to Kishkindha where his suspicions turned to certainty when he found that his brother had already assumed kingship of Kishkindha. 'Traitor,' shouted Vali and rushed towards his brother determined to kill him. Sugriva immediately realized there had been a misunderstanding. He tried to explain but Vali was in no mood to listen. Vali convinced himself that Sugriva always had his eye on being the sole ruler of Kishkindha and had plotted to kill him. He chased Sugriva all through the forest,

Devdutt Pattanaik

intent on killing him. And he would surely have succeeded had Sugriva not taken refuge on the hill called Rishyamukha. This was one place in Kishkindha that Vali feared to enter. For it was home to Matanga, a sage who had cursed Vali that if he ever stepped on the hill he would die instantly.

When Ram and Sugriva are introduced by Hanuman, Sugriva shows Ram jewels that he and his monkeys had found on the forest floor. Ram recognizes them as Sita's. Lakshman recognizes only Sita's anklets for he had all his life seen only his sister-in-law's feet—yet another indicator of Lakshman's chaste character. By contrast, Sugriva informs Ram that his brother, Vali, has forced his wife, Ruma, to become part of his harem.

Vali subscribes to the law of the jungle and so uses force to drive his brother away and lays claim to all the land and even his brother's wife. Even Ravana, by claiming Lanka by force, subscribes to the law of the jungle. Jungle law is known in Sanskrit as matsya nyaya or the law of fishes, where big fish eat the small fish. In the forest, the strong dominate the weak. By contrast, in the civilized world governed by dharma the weak need to be protected through laws. In a world of dharma, represented by Ayodhya, brothers share with each other. In the world of adharma, represented by Kishkindha and Lanka, brothers steal from each other.

Sugriva is eager to make friends with Ram. He offers to rescue Sita provided Ram kills Vali and makes him king of Kishkindha. It seems rather odd that Ram will stoop to such a transaction. Odder still is the way in which Vali is killed.

Death of Vali

Sugriva challenged Vali to a duel. The plan was that while Sugriva distracted his brother thus, Ram would shoot an arrow from behind the bushes and kill Vali. Unfortunately, when the two started fighting, Ram could not distinguish between the two brothers. Sugriva was thrashed and he ran back to Rishyamukha to save his life. When Ram explained what had happened, Sugriva with great reluctance agreed to challenge Vali once more to a fight, but this time he went with a garland of forest flowers round his neck. Vali, eager to kill his brother, pinned Sugriva to the ground and was about to snap his neck when Ram released his arrow that ripped through Vali's chest. 'Unfair. Unfair,' cried

Devdutt Pattanaik

Vali. Ram replied, 'All this land that I walk upon is the land ruled by Bharata and in all the land ruled by Bharata there must be dharma. You, Vali, who believe might is right, do not subscribe to dharma and so must be killed. He who lives by the law of the jungle must not object when he is killed by the law of the jungle.'

Vali is killed using the very laws he used to make himself king. Ram now demands that a new set of laws be established, one based not on power and domination but on love and generosity. Thus Ram becomes the harbinger of civilized conduct. He supports Sugriva only when he is convinced that as king, Sugriva will abandon the law of the jungle and embrace dharma. So while Vali behaves like an alpha male, driving Sugriva out and claiming his wife, Ruma, Ram insists that Sugriva treat Vali's wife, Tara, with respect and even declare Vali's son, Angad, as his heir. Had Sugriva still subscribed to the law of the jungle, he would have killed Vali's son and forced Tara to be his concubine.

But shortly after becoming king, Sugriva slips back into his animal instinct. He forgets that the foremost principle of dharma is to keep one's word. For this lapse, he is severely reprimanded by Lakshman.

Monsoons

After the death of Vali, Sugriva was made king of Kishkindha. He promised Ram to uphold dharma in his kingdom and accordingly accepted Vali's widow, Tara, as his wife and Vali's son, Angad, as his heir. It was decided to wait for the rainy season to pass before starting the search for Sita for during the rainy season the ground is slippery and treacherous and movement is impossible. Ram waited patiently for the rains to pass. When autumn arrived, Ram expected Sugriva to start the search for Sita. Unfortunately, Sugriva was lost in merrymaking following his coronation and had forgotten all about his promise to Ram. A furious Lakshman strode into the monkey king's palace to teach Sugriva a lesson. The merrymaking stopped and a terrified Sugriva hid behind the throne while Tara went to Lakshman and pacified him. A chastised Sugriva immediately summoned all the monkeys of the forest and ordered them to scour all four directions of the earth and not return until one of them found Sita.

Devdutt Pattanaik

In Lanka, Ravana's brothers who supported him when he drove Kuber away, refuse to support him when he abducts Sita. Both Vibhishana and Kumbhakarna feel what Ravana is doing is not right. Sita is another man's wife. To desire her is ethically and morally wrong, especially when she is clearly resisting. That being said, when Sita's husband finally launches a campaign to rescue his wife, Ravana's two brothers respond quite differently to the situation. Vibhishana simply parts ways with his brother but Kumbhakarna continues to stand by his brother.

Vibhishana

One day, the monkeys saw a Rakshasa flying through the air coming towards them. They ran and told Ram about him. Lakshman raised his bow ready to ward off any attack but Hanuman stopped him. He recognized the Rakshasa. It was Vibhishana, Ravana's younger brother. Hanuman had seen him argue against his brother's actions and being put down for it. 'I tried to make Ravana see sense. I told him it is adharma to hold captive another man's wife against her wishes. But he kicked me out of his court. Though he is my brother, I will not support this action of his. Therefore I have left Lanka and have decided to join you. Call me a traitor, but dharma is more important,' the Rakshasa said. Ram welcomed Vibhishana, touched by his willingness to sacrifice his own brother for a righteous cause.

Ravana has no qualms about endangering the life of Kumbhakarna. Despite this Kumbhakarna stands by Ravana. While Kumbhakarna does not agree with Ravana's immoral actions, he refuses to abandon his brother in a crisis.

Kumbhakarna's slumber

Ravana's brother, Kumbhakarna, was a powerful giant, feared by gods, demons and humans. Like Ravana, he had invoked Brahma with his austerities with the intention of asking for Indra's seat. Alarmed by this intention, Indra had begged Saraswati, goddess of speech, to twist Kumbhakarna's tongue so that instead of asking for Indra's seat he asked for Nidra's seat, which means the seat of the goddess of sleep, which means a bed. 'So be it,' said Brahma. 'You will sleep all the time.' Realizing what was happening,

Ravana begged Brahma to change his boon. 'How can you let him sleep all the time?' Brahma said, 'What is done cannot be undone. But I shall modify it. One day a year, Kumbhakarna shall awake. On that day he will be invincible. However, should he be roused on any other day, he will surely die.' So it came to pass, that Kumbhakarna spent all his life, except one day a year, asleep. When Ram attacked Lanka, and turned out to be a formidable opponent, a desperate Ravana decided to rouse Kumbhakarna from his sleep. 'He can destroy all the monkeys with a single sweep of his hand,' he said, forgetting Brahma's warning that the day Kumbhakarna's sleep would be interrupted would be the day of Kumbhakarna's death. Drums were beaten and conch-shells blown and a great din created to awaken Kumbhakarna. He was prodded with sharp tools, beaten with sticks and even kicked by elephants but he refused to wake up. Finally, vast vats of the best food were brought into his chambers. The aroma of the feast was so intense that Kumbhakarna's mouth watered and he woke up. While wolfing down his meal, Ravana apprised him of the situation. 'I don't agree with what you have done, brother. Nevertheless, I shall not turn against you as Vibhishana did. I shall fight for you because you are my brother.' So saying Kumbhakarna entered the battlefield and spread mayhem amongst the monkeys. He crushed them under his foot as if they were insects and he swatted them away like flies. The Vanaras began to flee and the Rakshasas began to cheer; then Ram entered the battlefield. Kumbhakarna saw Vibhishana stand next to Ram. 'Traitor,' he shouted and rushed towards him in a murderous rage. Ram, unperturbed by the sight of his gigantic monster, raised his bow and released his arrow. The missile hit its mark and Kumbhakarna fell down instantly.

Ravana broke down on hearing of Kumbhakarna's death. Unlike Ram who broke down when Lakshman was struck by an arrow, Ravana's sorrow has more to do with his imminent defeat than with the loss of his brother.

Through the characters of Kumbhakarna and Vibhishana, the *Ramayana* raises the question: What is more important, family loyalty or dharma? The answer given is clear enough: dharma is superior to loyalty. That is why Ram makes Vibhishana king of Lanka.

Having established dharma in Kishkindha and Lanka, Ram returns to Ayodhya. But before he steps in, he confirms if Bharata still upholds dharma or has he changed his mind.

Last chance for Bharata

Fourteen years had passed. It was time for Ram to return. But what if Bharata had changed his mind in this time? What if he did not want Ram to return? What if he wanted to be king of Ayodhya himself? So Ram sent Hanuman ahead of him, disguised as a Brahman, to check if Bharata truly wanted Ram to return and reclaim the crown. Hanuman found Bharata living like a hermit outside Ayodhya in the village of Nandigram serving as Ram's regent. Ram's sandals were still placed on the throne. 'Are you sure you want your brother to return?' asked Hanuman. 'You have a right to the throne. This could be your last chance to change your mind.' 'I have no intention of doing so,' said Bharata firmly. Hanuman persisted, offering many arguments for why Bharata and not Ram should rule Ayodhya.

Bharata refuted them all. 'Stop. No matter how hard you try I will not change my mind. Only Ram shall be king of Ayodhya,' said Bharata, convincing Hanuman of his sincerity. Hanuman then revealed his true identity and pointed to the sky. There, emerging from the clouds, was the flying chariot carrying Ram, Sita and Lakshman. Bharata saluted Ram and wept tears of joy. The unhappy days of Ayodhya were finally over.

After Ram becomes king, Lakshman's love and loyalty towards his brother is severely tested. In response to street gossip, Lakshman is asked by Ram to take Sita out of Ayodhya and leave her in the forest. He protests but finally obeys. Thus he survives a moral crisis, by staying loyal to his brother.

But in the end, circumstances force Lakshman to realize that there are times when, despite love for his brother, he has to disobey him for a greater good.

Lakshman disobeys

One day Kala, god of time, paid a visit to Ram and insisted that they talk in complete privacy. 'Anyone who tries to disturb this meeting should be killed,' Ram told Lakshman as he shut the door of his chambers. Lakshman stood guard to ensure no one disturbed Ram. At exactly that moment, the Rishi Durvasa stormed towards Ram's chambers. 'I want to see Ram immediately,' he demanded. Lakshman tried to explain that Ram did not want to be disturbed but Durvasa refused to take no for an answer. 'If you don't let me see Ram right now I shall curse him and his kingdom,' shouted the sage who was infamous for his temper. Not wanting any harm to befall Ram or Ayodhya, and not wanting to hurt Durvasa, Lakshman decided it was in everyone's best interest that he himself disturb Ram and inform him of Durvasa's presence. Later when Durvasa and Kala had left, Lakshman informed Ram that it was time for him to die for Ram had said anyone who disturbed his meeting with Kala had to be killed. Ram could not take back his word and Lakshman could not disobey his brother. So the two parted ways and Lakshman walked into the Sarayu river and gave up his mortal body.

While the *Ramayana* celebrates Lakshman's love for Ram, it also reminds us that ultimately, greater than any brother's love, greater than family, greater than anything in fact, is dharma, the code of civilized conduct, where others matter more than one's own.

6

Hanuman's Master

Ram, who is served by Hanuman
Ram, who promised to help Sugriva
Ram, who killed the proud Vali
Ram, who sent monkeys all over the world
Ram, who was consoled by Lakshman

—From the *Nama Ramayana*, which narrates the entire epic through the chanting of the many titles of Ram

Monkey to God

In north India there is a saying: pehle Hanuman, phir Bhagwan, first Hanuman, then God. Though a monkey, Hanuman, is one of the most widely worshipped gods in India. With no sophisticated philosophy associated with him, he is simply sankat mochan, the remover of problems, whose image stands alone in roadside shrines at crossroads, at entrances of cities, citadels, temples and homes. Though beast, he embodies all the qualities that make a human worthy of adoration: humility, strength and wisdom. And in a caste-based feudal society like India, Hanuman who stands outside the temple facing the street seems more accessible to the masses than his distant master, the royal Ram.

The word for monkey in the *Ramayana*, Vanara, is said to be derived from 'vana' meaning forest and 'nara' meaning man. Many have therefore argued that the monkeys referred to in the *Ramayana* are not actually monkeys but forest tribes who either worshipped monkeys or had monkeys as their symbols or behaved like monkeys. Vali, for example, behaves like an alpha male monkey who keeps all the foraging grounds and female monkeys for himself. Sugriva and his troupe represent the troop of exiled bachelor-monkeys driven away by the alpha male who continue to hover around the harem waiting for an opportunity to outsmart the leader. Of all the monkeys, Ram is drawn to one in particular, one who though an animal demonstrates better behaviour than the best of men. That monkey is Hanuman. Ram first encounters Hanuman in the forest when he enters Kishkindha in search of Sugriva and is suspected of being Vali's spy.

Hanuman meets Ram

When Ram and Lakshman entered Kishkindha, they met a Brahman who addressed them in chaste Sanskrit. The brothers were impressed and suspicious for they found it difficult to believe that a man with such diction, such deep knowledge of grammar and language would wander so far away from civilization in the forest said to be the home of monkeys. Lakshman was convinced that the Brahman, like the golden deer, was a shape-shifting Rakshasa. Ram refused to let past experience colour his judgement. He introduced himself to the Brahman as the son of Dashratha, king of Ayodhya, duty-bound to live in the forest as a hermit for fourteen years. He explained how his search for his missing wife had brought him to Kishkindha. The Brahman immediately revealed his true form: he was a mighty monkey called Hanuman, adviser to Sugriva. He had been sent by his master to find out who Ram and Lakshman were. 'You look like warriors but dress like hermits. So we did not know what to make of you. My master feared that you could have been sent by his brother, Vali, to hunt him down.'

Hanuman is no ordinary monkey. He is the son of Vayu, the wind god who could fly anywhere he wished. As a child he knew no fear, much to the exasperation of the other gods.

Eating the sun

As a child, Hanuman flew towards the rising sun mistaking it for a succulent fruit. On the way, he tossed the planets and the stars as if they were toys, annoying Indra, king of the sky, who struck him with a thunderbolt.

Later the sages decided that he should forget his great powers and remember that only when they were needed most. Hanuman was given the task of protecting Sugriva by his teacher, Surya, the sun god.

Hanuman's teacher

Hanuman wanted the sun god to be his teacher but Surya refused on grounds that all day he was busy travelling and all night he was busy resting. 'When can I stop to teach you?' he asked. 'You don't have to stop. Teach as you travel across the sky,' said Hanuman, who then expanded his size, placed one foot on the eastern mountains and another on the western mountains and kept facing the blazing sun god's chariot as it made its way each day from the eastern horizon to the western horizon. Impressed by Hanuman's persistence, Surya taught Hanuman all that he knew and that was a lot, for the sun sees the whole world and so has knowledge of the whole world. 'What shall I give you as fee?' asked Hanuman. Surya replied,

'My son, Sugriva, is suffering greatly at the hands
of his half-brother, Vali. Take care of him for me,' he
said. Hanuman promised to take care of Sugriva
but he refused to hurt Vali because Vali was the
son of Indra.

Hanuman helps Sugriva form an alliance with
Ram. This alliance helps Sugriva become king of the
monkeys. An indebted Sugriva orders his monkeys to
scour the earth for Sita. Search parties are sent in every
direction. The best of monkeys are sent to the south,
the direction that Ravana was last seen travelling with
Sita. The search party is headed by Sugriva's nephew,
Angad. This despite the fact that Hanuman, who
follows Angad, is clearly more powerful. Hanuman has
no issues being Angad's follower. This is Hanuman's
personality—always a team player, ever willing to
serve, with absolutely no desire to dominate.

Before the journey begins, Hanuman displays his
foresight which doubles Ram's admiration for him.

Hanuman's foresight

'If I find Sita,' said Hanuman, 'how will I convince
her that I have indeed been sent by you?' Impressed
by Hanuman's foresight, Ram gave him his ring.

'Show this to her and she will know you are my messenger.'

Though Angad is the leader, it is Hanuman who ensures that the monkeys are not distracted from their mission.

Swayamprabha

Angad was given the task of searching the southern direction, where Lanka stood in all probability. For days they travelled through forests and over hills and across deserts but they found no trace of Lanka or Ravana or Sita. Finally they entered a cave. The dark cave led them to a great magical city full of delightful things. All the monkeys were enchanted by the things there. 'Stay and enjoy this wonderful place forever,' said Swayamprabha, guardian of the magical city, 'for you cannot leave this cave alive.' Hanuman, who was part of this group, stopped the monkeys from enjoying the tempting things before them. 'We are on a mission,' he reminded them. He then begged Swayamprabha to let them go. He told her the tale of Sita's abduction. Impressed by the sincerity and selflessness of Hanuman, Swayamprabha transported the monkeys to the southernmost tip of India. Beyond lay the southern sea. Beyond that stood the golden city of Lanka.

When faced with an apparent dead end, Angad becomes nervous and agitated.

Sampati

Angad's heart sank when he saw the vast ocean. This he believed was the southern end of the world. Where was Lanka then, he wondered. 'We cannot go back without finding Lanka or Sita. Sugriva will kill us,' he said. In despair, he decided to sit on the beach and starve himself to death. An old vulture called Sampati overheard Angad's intention and hopped towards them. 'I will eat you when you are dead,' he said. Ignoring him, Angad moaned, 'Had Jatayu not told Ram that he saw Ravana move in the southern direction, we would not have had to bear the maximum burden of finding Sita.' Hearing Jatayu's name, Sampati was intrigued, for Sampati was Jatayu's brother. They were both sons of Arun, god of dawn. They once got into a competition of reaching the sun first. Sampati flew ahead of Jatayu and got his wings singed so badly that he tumbled and fell on the southern beach unable to fly ever again. On learning how Ravana had killed Jatayu, Sampati decided to avenge his brother's death by revealing the whereabouts of Lanka. Though he could not fly, Sampati had keen eyesight and could see beyond the southern horizon. He strained his eyes and said, 'I can see the island of Trikuta and on it the golden city of Lanka and in it a garden where under a tree sits an unhappy woman. She must be Sita.' He told the monkeys the exact direction and distance to Lanka, for which the monkeys were grateful.

While Angad gets stressed, Hanuman discovers his inner strength that enables him to cross the sea to Lanka.

Hanuman's strength

The monkeys wondered how they would cross the sea and reach Lanka. 'We can't jump that far,' they said. Jambavan, a bear who had joined the monkeys looking for Sita, said, 'Hanuman can. Even he does not realize his strength. As a child, he had leapt towards the sun and tried to eat it as if it was a fruit. He had tossed the planets around as if they were toys. Indra had to stop him by hurling his thunderbolt. As he fell to the ground, the gods gave him many powers but the sages decreed that he would never realize them until the time was right. That time is now. Have faith in Ram, Hanuman. With him in mind, leap and you shall be able to cross the sea.' Hanuman meditated on Ram and was able to discover his latent powers. He increased his size till his head reached the sky. Then climbing a hillock, he leapt up into the sky and made his way across the sea cheered by Jambavan, Angad and all the other monkeys.

Hanuman's journey to Lanka is an eventful one described in detail in the Sundarkand of Valmiki's *Ramayana*. He does not stop to rest, even when an undersea mountain rises up to offer him shelter. With cunning, he outwits Surasa while with brute strength he overpowers both Simhika and Lankini.

Journey across the sea

As he made his way through the sky across the sea, Hanuman encountered many obstacles.

Surasa, a sea serpent, blocked his path and said that she was hungry and she would not let Hanuman pass until he entered her mouth. Hanuman expanded himself in size forcing Surasa to stretch her mouth wide. Then, in the blink of an eye, he reduced himself to the size of a bee and darted in and out of Surasa's mouth. Impressed by his cunning, Surasa blessed Hanuman as he continued on his journey. Then another demoness called Simhika caught Hanuman by pinning down his shadow with magic. As she dragged him towards her, Hanuman kicked her hard and killed her. The mountain Mainaka rose from the depths of the ocean and invited Hanuman to rest on its peak. Hanuman refused as he was on a mission. Finally, Hanuman reached the shores of Lanka. There he encountered Lankini, the guardian goddess of the city of Lanka. They fought and Hanuman succeeded in overpowering her. This was a bad omen for Lanka for with its guardian goddess overpowered by a monkey its days were clearly numbered.

The scriptures constantly allude to the fact that Hanuman is celibate. His overpowering of three female forces—Surasa, Simhika and Lankini—reinforces his potent masculinity. One folk narrative has it that while crossing over to Lanka, Hanuman's sweat fell into the sea. That sweat was eaten by a fish. So potent was Hanuman's sweat that the fish gave birth to a child whose name was Makaradhvaj.

In Lanka, Hanuman finds many women. He identifies Sita on the principle that Ram's wife would never derive any pleasure from the luxuries provided by her abductor.

Finding Sita

Hanuman searched every house in Lanka looking for Sita. He found Ravana in bed with hundreds of women. A few of them were his wives, a few were his concubines and many were wives of other men who had come to him willingly drawn by his power. Hanuman was sure Sita was not amongst them. He then saw a beautiful woman sleeping alone in the palace. She was bedecked in bridal finery. Hanuman concluded that she was Ravana's chief queen and not Sita for Ram's wife would never enjoy the pleasures of another man's palace. He then reached an orchard where under the Ashoka tree he found a forlorn woman seated, surrounded by fierce Rakshasa women. He saw Ravana come into the orchard with all royal fanfare. Using gifts and threats and sweet words, he tried to make the woman come to him but she firmly turned him down. This convinced Hanuman that the woman in the orchard was indeed Sita. After Ravana had left, he climbed the tree under which Sita sat and began to sing songs to Ram's glory. That caught Sita's attention. He then dropped Ram's ring before her. She recognized it at once. Still she looked suspiciously at him. Hanuman then revealed his identity and told Sita how Ram had taken the help of the monkeys of Kishkindha to locate her. He offered to carry Sita across the sea to Ram. But Sita refused. 'My husband is a warrior. Ravana has insulted him by treating his wife so. Let him regain his lost pride by defeating Ravana in battle and releasing me with honour.' Hanuman understood Sita's viewpoint and requested her to give him something that would prove to Ram that he had indeed established contact with her. Sita pulled out her hairpin and gave it to Hanuman. 'He will recognize this,' she said. Hanuman then fell at her feet and sought her blessings which Sita gave freely for Hanuman's arrival had reinforced her hope.

Hanuman could have left after delivering the message, but the monkey in him could not resist the chance of teaching Ravana a lesson.

Burning of Lanka

Having located Sita, Hanuman could have returned to Ram but he decided not to do so until he had taught Ravana a lesson. He started leaping from tree to tree in the garden where Sita was held prisoner, breaking the branches and destroying the flowers and fruits. When the Rakshasa guards tried to stop him, he threw stones at them. One of the stones hit Ravana's son, Akshay, and killed him. An alarm was sounded across the palace and Indrajit, Ravana's eldest and mightiest of sons, was forced to come to the garden and catch the wild monkey. Indrajit released a missile imbuing its tip with the power of Brahma. Out of respect for Brahma, Hanuman let the missile entrap him. Hanuman was immediately tied and dragged before Ravana.

When asked to identify himself, Hanuman split the chains that bound him as if they were made of straw, announced himself as the messenger of Ram and demanded a seat for himself. Ravana was surprised to hear Ram's name in his court and annoyed by the monkey's superior attitude. Hanuman refused to speak any more until he was given a seat due to a royal messenger. When none was forthcoming, he simply elongated his tail and coiled it around to create a very high and impressive seat for himself. Sitting on it, he informed Ravana of Ram's imminent arrival. 'Let Sita go or face his wrath,' he warned the king of the Rakshasas. A furious Ravana ordered his guards to set fire to Hanuman's tail. When this was done, Hanuman simply swung his tail and leapt from one corner of the palace to another and then from one roof to another setting all of Lanka aflame. After causing maximum damage to the city of the Rakshasas, Hanuman made his way back across the sea.

Having located Sita for Ram, Hanuman then organizes all the monkeys to build a bridge to Lanka.

Bridge to Lanka

Having located Sita in Lanka, Sugriva ordered that an army be raised to rescue her. 'But how will we get to Lanka which is an island in the middle of the sea? Not all of us are like Hanuman, capable of flying so far,' wondered the monkeys. On reaching the southern shore, Ram raised his bow and threatened the sea with a deadly arrow if it did not make way for his army. Varun, god of the sea, appeared before Ram and begged him not to release the arrow. 'Build a bridge instead with stones. And I will ensure that all sea creatures keep your stones afloat,' he said. Directed by Hanuman, all the monkeys collected rocks to build the bridge to Lanka. On each rock Hanuman engraved the name of Ram so that the god of the sea could identify the rocks easily and keep them afloat.

Besides getting Ram's army across to Lanka, Hanuman is also credited with saving Lakshman's life.

Indrajit strikes Lakshman

Ravana's eldest son Indrajit was also called Meghnad because when he was born his cry sounded like thundering clouds. He grew up well versed in serpent lore known as Naga-shastra and even married a serpent princess called Sulochana. He challenged and defeated Indra himself in a duel and so came to be known as Indrajit. After a long fight, he was able to strike Lakshman with a serpent arrow. With a triumphant laugh, he withdrew while Lakshman lay dying on the battlefield. Ram watched in horror as the poison spread through his brother's limbs. 'I have failed in my duty as elder brother. I have failed to protect my younger brother,' wailed Ram as he gathered Lakshman's limp body in his arms. Watching Ram suffer so, Vibhishana said there was a way to rescue Lakshman. There was an antidote to the poison spreading through Lakshman's limbs. It was a herb called sanjivani located in a mountain far away in the north. If given before sunrise, Lakshman could be saved. 'I shall fetch it,' said Hanuman and leapt northwards at lightning speed. On reaching the mountain, Hanuman realized he could not identify the herb described by Vibhishana. So he picked up the entire mountain and carried it back to the battlefield. Vibhishana scoured the

Devdutt Pattanaik

mountain, found the herb, prepared the potion which Ram poured into Lakshman's mouth. The antidote worked and Lakshman woke up as if from a deep slumber just before sunrise, eager to resume his battle with Indrajit.

According to one Ram-katha, Ravana forced Surya to rise earlier than usual in order to thwart Hanuman's efforts to bring the magic herb before sunrise. Realizing this, Hanuman simply grabbed the sun god and trapped him under his armpit. Such was his strength.

Later Hanuman disrupts Indrajit's ritual making it possible for Lakshman to defeat Indrajit.

Death of Indrajit

Indrajit had obtained from Brahma a boon—that he would die only at the hands of a man who had not slept for fourteen years. When he learnt that Lakshman was such a man, he became nervous. His anxiety increased when Lakshman survived despite being shot by the deadly serpent arrow. So Indrajit decided to perform an occult ritual that would render him invincible. When Vibhishana learnt of Indrajit's plans, he directed Hanuman and the other monkeys to the secret chambers where he knew the ritual would be performed. Led by Hanuman, the monkeys disrupted the yagna. Indrajit could do nothing but watch helplessly and curse his treacherous uncle. The following day, Indrajit entered the battlefield, a little disappointed and angry and extremely nervous. He came face to face with Lakshman and a great battle ensued. Missiles were hurled and struck down by either side. At long last, Lakshman was able to release a powerful arrow that escaped being struck down; it severed Indrajit's neck with such force that it carried the head straight into Ravana's palace.

Hanuman's story clearly delights everyone who reads the *Ramayana*. He is Ram's knight. With him around, everyone feels safe and secure. But underneath his great adventures is a philosophy that transforms this swashbuckling monkey into a much-venerated deity.

After the defeat of Ravana, Hanuman leaves the monkeys and follows Ram to Ayodhya. There, in the land of Manavas, he displays his absolute devotion to Ram.

Hanuman's heart

During Ram's coronation, a pearl necklace was given to Hanuman. The people of Ayodhya saw Hanuman examining each pearl carefully and then throwing it away. 'Don't you know the value of a pearl, you stupid monkey,' said the people of Ayodhya. 'A pearl has no value,' said Hanuman, 'if it does not have Ram's name or image on it. 'By that logic, even your body has no value because it does not have Ram's name or image on it,' said the people. 'Who says so?' asked Hanuman. With his bare nails he tore open his chest. Within, on his heart, the people of Ayodhya were amazed to find the image of Ram and Sita.

Hanuman's appeal comes from the fact that he is not the beneficiary of any of his adventures. All his life is dedicated to others—first Sugriva, then Ram. He is a celibate ascetic. This celibacy generates tapa which manifests as his strength and his intellect. His ascetic nature is reinforced by folk narratives that insist that he is an aspect of Shiva, the supreme hermit.

Birth of Hanuman

Once Vishnu took the form of Mohini, an enchantress. So beautiful was Mohini that even

Shiva, the ascetic, was enchanted by her. Unable to control his senses, Shiva shed semen that was collected by Vayu, the wind god. He poured it into the ear of Anjana, the wife of Kesari, a monkey. This made Anjana pregnant and she gave birth to Hanuman.

Not only is Hanuman a powerful monkey who burnt Lanka, he is also a poet, a grammarian and a scholar. Despite all these qualities he is content sitting at Ram's feet as his servant. It is said that Hanuman is present every time the *Ramayana* is narrated. That is why even today, during the narration of the *Ramayana*, an empty seat is kept in his honour.

In art, monkeys are a symbol of the mind, since both are innately restless and curious. When a problem appears to the mind as an insurmountable mountain, the monkey-like mind can, through devotion and discipline, transform into Hanuman and fly with the mountain-like problem in hand.

Devdutt Pattanaik

7

Ravana's Enemy

He who does not desire the wife or wealth of others
He who is not jealous of others' fame or prosperity
He who always is interested in doing good to others
I seek the protection
Of that lotus-eyed boon of the Raghu clan

—From the prayer of Jatayu in *Adhyatma*
Ramayana

Descent of man

With ten heads and twenty arms, riding a flying chariot, Ravana makes an impressive opponent. He is the lord of the Rakshasas, ruler of the golden city of Lanka, located on the island of Trikuta in the middle of the southern sea.

While his mother was Kaikesi, a Rakshasa woman, his father was a Brahman. Not any ordinary Brahman — a Rishi named Vishrava, son of Pulastya, who was one of the seven primal sages, just like Vasishtha, created by Brahma himself to be the guardian of Vedic lore.

In the varna hierarchy, Ravana, a Brahman, holds a higher rank than Ram, who is a Kshatriya. That is why it is said that after killing Ravana, Ram went to Rishikesh and performed a penance to rid himself of Brahma-hatya-paap, the crime of killing a learned soul. The story goes that before Ravana died, Ram even accepted him as a teacher.

Ravana, the teacher

As a mortally wounded Ravana lay on the ground moaning and groaning, Ram told Lakshman to go to him and gather as much knowledge as he could for Ravana, though a Rakshasa, was also a Rishi's son, and a great scholar. Lakshman went to Ravana and standing next to his head said, 'Ravana! Struck by Ram's arrow you will surely die. But before you go, share your knowledge so that it will outlive you.' Ravana did not reply, he simply turned his face away. Lakshman went to his brother and informed him that Ravana was not being cooperative. 'Where did you stand while addressing him?' asked Ram. 'Near his head. Why?' asked Lakshman. 'If you want him to teach you, the least you can do is behave like a student.' So Ram walked up to Ravana and sat near his feet. 'Noble king of the Rakshasas, for the crime you committed against me you have been punished. I have no ill feelings towards you at this moment. Only great regard for your wisdom. I, seated at your feet as a student, humbly request you to share your knowledge with me.' Ravana smiled and looked at Lakshman who lowered his eyes in shame.

'Ram, you are truly a worthy opponent and the noblest being on earth, able to detach yourself from your emotions. I salute you. I have little time before I die. But I shall teach you what I consider the most important lesson of my life. Remember, it is the nature of the ignorant mind to be drawn towards things that will cause harm and to avoid things that are good. We must remember that what tempts us will in all probability be the cause of our downfall. What we shy away from, what we procrastinate about, probably is what will help us evolve.' So saying, Ravana breathed his last. And Ram bowed his head to his teacher.

Ravana is revered as a great devotee of Shiva. He designed a lute in honour of Shiva called the Rudra-veena using one of his heads as the gourd, his arm as the beam, his nerves as the strings. He composed a hymn for Shiva called the Rudra-stotra. Shiva considered him to be the greatest of his devotees and offered him many boons. But the boons asked by Ravana reveal his personality. The following story forms the theme of a Kuchipudi dance recital.

Mandodari

Shiva once asked Ravana what he wanted. Ravana replied, 'I want to marry your wife.' Shiva, the guileless ascetic, gave his assent. Shiva's consort, Shakti, did not blame her husband—she realized Ravana had taken advantage of his innocence. She had to remedy the situation herself. So she took a frog and turned her into a nymph. Ravana saw the nymph and assumed that she had to be Parvati. Which other damsel would live on the icy slopes of Mount Kailas with Shiva, he thought. Ravana took the damsel to Lanka and made her his queen. She was called Mandodari after manduka, the frog.

Shiva embodies the principle of vairagya, absolute detachment. Yet, Ravana, his greatest devotee, is fully attached to worldly things. He wants what others have. He even wants what Shiva has. He displays not an ounce of humility. In his pride, he believes he is more powerful than Shiva himself. The following story forms the theme of many temple wall carvings such as those in Ellora and Elephanta.

Moving Kailas

Ravana felt the journey from Lanka, in the south, to Shiva's abode, Mount Kailas, in the north, was too long and tedious. So he decided to uproot Kailas and carry it closer to Lanka. Shiva found the whole enterprise very amusing. But as the mountain rose and Kailas shook, Shiva's terrified children, Ganesh and Kartik, began to cry. Shiva's wife, Parvati, begged him to stop Ravana. Shiva realized that what Ravana was doing was wrong. So he pressed his big toe gently on the mountain creating such force that Ravana buckled under the pressure and the entire Mount Kailas came crashing down on him.

Ravana uses his immense power to assert his authority over land. He drives his brother Kuber away from Lanka and usurps his throne. Ravana also uses his power to force himself upon women. Some women, wives of other men, come to him voluntarily leaving their husbands behind, drawn by his beauty and charm and power. Other women are simply forced to be part of his harem. When Hanuman enters Lanka he finds Ravana in bed with many beautiful women, all of them are smitten by his virile power. But there were women who refused to submit to Ravana. One was Vedavati.

Vedavati

When Ravana tried to molest a hermit woman called Vedavati she leapt into the fire declaring her intention to be the cause of Ravana's death in her next life.

In the fifteenth-century *Anand Ramayana*, the woman who rejects Ravana is Padmaksha, an incarnation of the goddess Lakshmi herself. Sita is said to be one of these wronged women reborn. Sita exists solely to be the cause of Ravana's destruction. She is Ram's wife but the object of Ravana's lust. She is bound to Ram by rules but Ravana craves her in passion. All human beings can behave either as Ram or Ravana, obeying or disregarding the rules, because Ram and Ravana represent two ends of the human spectrum.

Ram stands for dharma, Ravana stands for adharma. Ram stands for intellect, Ravana stands for instinct. Ram stands for the soul, Ravana stands for the ego. Ram stands for love, Ravana for power. Ram is the best of the Manavas, Ravana is the worst of the Rakshasas. Ram is therefore God while Ravana is a demon. Confrontation between them is inevitable.

When Ravana learns of Ram from his sister, he becomes insecure. Ram is everything he is not. Ram does not submit to passion. Even in the forest, where there are no rules, he is disciplined enough to be faithful to his wife. Surpanakha knows that the self-indulgent Ravana will not fight Ram only to avenge her humiliation. That would be expecting too much of him. So she stirs lust in him, thereby making the abduction of Sita as much about satisfying his passions as it is about avenging Surpanakha.

Since Ravana subscribes to the law of the jungle where all is fair, he does not shy away from using cunning to get his hands on Sita. It is only within civilization where dharma holds sway that trickery and cunning are frowned upon. In the forest, animals use cunning in the quest for survival. Ravana, however, uses cunning for his own pleasure.

Maricha

Ravana decided to abduct Sita. 'Do not fight the brothers,' warned Maricha. 'I have encountered them long ago while they were defending Vishwamitra's yagna. They possess powerful weapons. Use cunning.' So Ravana came up with a plan that would force Ram to leave Sita unguarded in the forest. He ordered Maricha to take the form of a golden deer and make himself visible to Sita. Sure enough, on seeing the golden deer, Sita told Ram, 'Fetch me that strange deer, dead or alive. Dead, I shall make clothes with its hide. Alive, I shall keep it as a pet.' To please Sita, Ram picked up his bow and chased the deer. The deer, sometimes appearing, sometimes disappearing, managed to lure Ram deep into the woods. When Ram finally struck him with an arrow, Maricha screamed mimicking Ram's voice, 'Help, Lakshman! Help!'

At first, Lakshman refuses to leave his sister-in-law. But Sita provokes him with an unthinkable thought. In order to force her will on Lakshman, Sita suggests a vile possibility that can only take place when dharma breaks down. Thus in insecurity and anxiety, Sita abandons dharma and that proves to be her undoing. Before leaving, Lakshman tries to salvage the situation by doing something that annoys Ravana greatly.

Lakshman Rekha

When Sita heard Ram's cry for help, she expected Lakshman to rush to his brother's rescue. Instead

Lakshman stood there bow in hand. 'Something is amiss. I don't believe Ram is in trouble. Anyway, he asked me to stay here and protect you. That is what I shall do.' Sita was furious at Lakshman's behaviour. 'Go,' she said, 'your brother needs you.' But Lakshman refuses to budge. Anxious for her husband, irritated by her brother-in-law's obstinacy, Sita said, 'Maybe you want something to happen to your brother. Then you can have your way with me.' Lakshman was horrified at such a suggestion. 'Then prove me wrong. Go help your brother,' Sita ordered. Lakshman immediately rushed in the direction the voice had come from. Before leaving he traced a line around the grass hut and said, 'Stay within these lines and you will be safe, for within is Ram's kingdom where you are Ram's wife and outside is the forest where such rules of dharma do not apply.'

Lakshman's line or Lakshman Rekha is the line of chastity. Outside the line, is the jungle, inside its boundaries, civilization. Outside, the law of the jungle applies and inside, dharma rules. Outside, Sita is a woman for the taking but inside she is Ram's wife, protected by the laws of marriage.

Ravana knows that if he crosses the line and forces himself upon Sita, it will be rape. But if he lures her outside, his abduction will not be governed by ethics and morals that govern human society. So he comes up with a plan that will force Sita to willingly cross Lakshman's line.

Abduction of Sita

As soon as Sita was alone, Ravana came to the grass hut disguised as an ascetic and asked Sita to serve him food. Sita invited the ascetic to come into her house and eat there. 'I cannot enter a house of a woman when she is alone. It is highly inappropriate. Come out and serve me,' said Ravana. So Sita collected whatever food she had inside the hut and stretched out her hand to serve the ascetic, taking care not to cross the line traced by Lakshman. 'Why do you stretch your arm so? This is highly inappropriate. Come forward and serve your guest appropriately,' demanded Ravana. Sita did not know what to do. She remembered her brother-in-law's words that she was safe only within the line. 'Why do you hesitate to feed me? What kind of a woman are you? Do you not know that to treat a guest so is

Devdutt Pattanaik

adharma? You should be cursed for this. No, your entire household, your husband and his entire family, should be cursed for this.' Alarmed, Sita stepped out of the grass hut and offered the food to the ascetic only to realize he was no ascetic. He was a Rakshasa. Ravana caught hold of Sita and dragged her to his flying chariot and made his way to Lanka.

Ravana cleverly puts Sita in a dilemma. As the wife of a Kshatriya warrior, she is obliged by dharma to take care of guests. She cannot do so if she stays within the line. In fact if she insists on staying within, she risks a curse on her husband's family. So, for the sake of dharma, she is forced to step out. Once out, she becomes a victim of jungle law. She is no longer Ram's wife. She is but a female creature that the most aggressive or the most cunning male can claim. Ravana does precisely that. By jungle law that states might is right, he has done nothing wrong.

Luckily Ram discovers the trail left behind by Sita. He learns she has been taken south.

That Lanka is located to the south is significant. This is not the geographical south as is conventionally believed. It is the metaphorical south. In Vastu-shastra or the occult science of space, the south is the direction of Yama or the god of decay and death making north the direction of growth and immortality. In the north is the Pole Star, symbol of stability and steadfastness. In the south everything is unstable and insecure. Ram moves from the north to the south to conquer the decay in human values embodied in Ravana. He will go into the forest and replace the law of the jungle with the code of civilization.

In his journey south, even before Sita's abduction, Ram keeps killing Rakshasas who actually turn out to be Gandharvas cursed to be demons, suggesting that the 'killings' are actually metaphors of transformation. Ram kills the followers of adharma so that they are reborn as the followers of dharma.

Viradha

While in the forest, a hideous demon called Viradha who had killed many animals carried Sita away. Ram and Lakshman confronted this demon and tried to kill him with their many weapons but none seemed to work on him. Viradha dropped Sita and picked Ram and Lakshman up as if they were children and carried them deep into the forest intent on eating them. The two brothers

broke his arms. Realizing he could not be killed by
weapons, they dug a pit and buried him alive. From
the pit arose a Gandharva who identified himself
as Tumburu cursed by Kuber, lord of the Yakshas,
to become a Rakshasa until he was liberated
by Ram.

Ram meets many animals in the forest who under
his influence start behaving differently. Their actions
are no longer motivated by the desire to survive. They
perform selfless deeds, acts of generosity even at the
cost of their own life.

Jatayu

Sita screamed for help as Ravana's flying chariot
made its way through the sky. Hearing this, the
vulture Jatayu rushed to her rescue and blocked
Ravana's path. A great fight followed. Ravana
finally raised his sword and chopped Jatayu's
wings. Jatayu tumbled down and could only watch
helplessly as the chariot of the Rakshasa-king
made its way south.

Ram treats Jatayu with great dignity. He addresses
him as father and cremates him as he would have

cremated his own father had he had the chance. Thus, under Ram's influence even a vulture, a creature that feeds on the dead, transforms into a creature willing to die for others.

Another Rakshasa is so happy to be killed by Ram that he transforms into a helpful Gandharva who advises Ram to makes allies with the monkeys of Kishkindha in his search for Sita.

Kabandha

As Ram and Lakshman moved south in search of Sita, they were caught by a demon that had no head or neck or legs. Just two extremely long arms and a torso. On the torso were one eye and a vast mouth lined with sharp teeth. This was Kabandha, who was once a Gandharva. But he had challenged Indra to a duel and Indra had struck him so hard with his thunderbolt that his head and his legs got squashed into his torso. Ram and Lakshman raised their bows and shot several arrows at the demon forcing him to release them. A mortally wounded Kabandha begged the brothers to set him on fire. As soon as the brothers did that, Kabandha emerged from the flames, his Gandharva form restored. As he rose towards the heavens, he advised Ram to take the help of the monkey Sugriva who lived in the forest of Kishkindha near lake Pampa next to the hill known as Rishyamukha. Sugriva had a good knowledge of geography and would know where Ravana's kingdom stood.

The kingdom of Kishkindha stands between Ayodhya and Lanka, between the land where the law of civilization is respected and the land where it is disregarded. The Vanaras thus stand between Manavas and Rakshasas.

In the beginning, the monkeys are aligned to the way of the jungle, like Ravana. Their leader Vali is described as mightier than Ravana. Once, Vali had caught Ravana by his tail and dragged him through Kishkindha like a dog on a leash. Like a creature aligned to the law of the jungle, Sugriva initially respects Ram only because Ram demonstrates that he is stronger than Ravana.

Display of Ram's strength

Sugriva showed Ram the carcass of a giant buffalo called Dundhubi that had been killed by Vali. After killing it, Vali had kicked it so hard that it had landed upon Rishyamukha hill. As it hit the ground, drops of its blood fell on a Rishi called Matanga who was meditating there. Furious, the sage had cursed Vali never to step upon mount Rishyamukha. 'If you can kick this carcass as far as Vali did, I will believe that you are as strong as Vali,' said Sugriva. So Ram kicked the carcass and to the astonishment of all the monkeys, it went up into the air and fell far away right in front of where Vali held court. Sugriva then said that Vali could uproot seven palm trees with one hand. If Ram could do the same, he would be sure that Ram was as strong as Vali. Ram pulled out an arrow and shot it with such force that it penetrated through all seven trees. These two acts of strength and skill convinced Sugriva that Ram would indeed make a worthy ally.

After killing Vali, Ram demands that the monkeys change their ways and subscribe to the code of civilization and help the weak. In dharma, one is expected to do things selflessly and out of generosity. When the monkeys help Ram to find Sita, they are doing it partly out of a sense of obligation and partly out of selflessness. Sugriva is keeping his word

Devdutt Pattanaik

to Ram. And this display of integrity is a sign that dharma has percolated into the monkey kingdom.

At the same time there is another monkey called Hanuman who, unlike Sugriva, is not bound by any obligation to serve Ram. He does so nevertheless. Hanuman is driven by devotion. He is selflessness personified. Hanuman even abandons the natural instincts of sex and violence—he becomes celibate and uses force only in the service of Ram. Hanuman thus represents the acme of transformation from beast to god. It is Hanuman who makes the perilous journey to Lanka and finds Sita.

Hanuman discovers that Ravana never forces himself upon Sita. Subplots of the *Ramayana* inform us that the demon-king is prevented from doing so either because of a curse or because Sita defends herself using the power of chastity. But at a more psychological level, a man like Ravana who loves to dominate those around him, would derive greater pleasure in making Sita come to him voluntarily in fear or in desire. Making a chaste wife abandon her faithful husband of her own free will would be for Ravana his ultimate triumph.

Ravana would like both Sita and Ram to become Rakshasas; Sita by submitting to her passions and

Ram by submitting to his rage and insecurity. To his great annoyance, neither abandon dharma. Despite all charms and threats, Sita remains the faithful wife. And her husband turns out to be a gentle, dignified and upright warrior.

Ravana can let Sita go and avert war, but despite advice from his brothers, his wives, his mother and father, he clings to her like a child refusing to part with his toy. It is both a matter of attachment and pride, a refusal to compromise for the sake of peace.

Without any qualms, he sacrifices the lives of his sons and his brothers, lets them all die, lets Lanka burn, but refuses to submit. This stubborn refusal to let Sita go and willingness to destroy others for his self-indulgence, is an indicator of his ego.

After all his relatives and soldiers have been killed, Ravana finally steps into the battlefield. This is no brave and proud king. This is an insecure man, all of whose attempts at self-preservation have failed.

In some tellings, Ram rides into battle on Hanuman's shoulders while in others Indra himself sends down his chariot for Ram. In some tellings, after a fierce battle, Ram releases a mighty weapon that strikes Ravana on his chest and kills him. In others, Vibhishana turns traitor and informs Ram of the secret of Ravana's apparent invincibility. In some Ram-kathas, clearly inspired by folk tales, Ravana's life is hidden in a wasp locked in a chest that Hanuman and Lakshman finally find after many adventures. The following retelling from the Telugu *Ranganatha Ramayana* shows how Ram refuses to take advantage of the secret information about Ravana's strength given to him by Vibhishana on grounds that it violates the code of dharma.

Ravana's navel

Ravana finally entered the battlefield. The monkeys and demons withdrew as Ram and Ravana came face to face. The gods gathered in the sky and the serpents arose under the earth to see this great battle. Both Ram and Ravana raised their bows. The fight was fierce. Ravana shot hundreds of arrows towards Ram. Ram shattered them with his own arrows before they even came near him. Ravana too destroyed arrows released by Ram. Ram's arrows did manage to cut one of Ravana's heads. But to his astonishment, the head replaced itself. 'Why is it so?' asked Ram. 'Because,' whispered Vibhishana, 'he has hidden a pot of amrit, the nectar of immortality, in his navel. Shoot him in the navel.' 'To shoot below an enemy's neck would be inappropriate,' said Ram, quoting the rules of war. He shot yet another arrow towards Ravana's chest. Hanuman then invoked his father, Vayu, the wind god, who caused a blast of breeze to suddenly appear on the battlefield and force Ram's arrow to change direction towards Ravana's navel. Escaping all of Ravana's attempts to stop it, the arrow pierced Ravana's navel. The hidden pot of amrit was shattered and all the nectar poured out. Deprived of its power, Ravana became a mortal. Ram's next arrow ripped through Ravana's chest. Blood gushed out and he fell to the ground letting out a spine-chilling roar. The wind stopped, the waters stilled, and everyone watched spellbound as the great king of the Rakshasas collapsed. After a moment of stunned silence, the monkeys led by Hanuman let out a cheer. 'Victory to Sita's Ram! Victory to Sita's Ram!' Vibhishana rushed to his brother's side and wept. But for Ravana's obduracy, this tragic end could have been averted.

Symbolically, the end of Ravana is the end of the basest of human instincts. Having killed Ravana, Ram returns with Sita to Ayodhya in the north, his mission on earth accomplished.

Return to Ayodhya

The war was won. The period of exile was over. It was time to return home. Vibhishana, now king of Lanka, advised Ram, Lakshman and Sita to return on Ravana's flying chariot. 'You have suffered so much. Let your return be comfortable.' And so Ram with Sita by his side along with Lakshman mounted the Pushpak viman. Hanuman requested that he be allowed to join them. Sugriva willingly gave his assent. As the Vanaras and Rakshasas cheered, the chariot rose to the sky and made its way north towards Ayodhya.

Ravana has ten pairs of eyes, which means he can see more. Ravana has ten sets of arms, which means he can do more. Ravana has ten heads, which means he can think more. And yet, this man with superior body and mind submits to the basest of passions. Despite having a full understanding of the soul indicated by his scholarship in the Vedas, despite knowing the futility of clinging to things material indicated by his adoration of Shiva, he submits to passion and surrenders to his ego.

He embodies the difficult journey from the head to the heart—from knowing to becoming. This journey from knowing to becoming is the journey of transformation from Ravana to Ram.

Devdutt Pattanaik

8

Ayodhya's King

King Ram
Chief of the Raghu clan
Uplifter of the fallen
Sita's Ram
Also known as God and Allah
Bless everyone with wisdom

— From Vishnu Digambar Paluskar's composition,
Raghupati Raghav Raja Ram, based on a hymn
by the seventeenth-century Marathi saint-poet
Ramdas

Resolving conflict

Manu, the son of Surya, the sun god, was the first king of mankind; he established the code of civilization that Hindus call dharma.

Manu had two sons, Ikshavaku and Ila. Some say Ila was a daughter, who married Mercury, the son of Chandra, the moon god. Descendants of Ikshavaku are identified as belonging to the solar line of kings or Surya-vamsa while the descendants of Ila are known as Chandra-vamsa, the lunar line of kings. The two royal lines produced leaders of different characters. While the solar line of kings became renowned for their moral uprightness, the lunar line of kings were known for their moral ambiguity.

Ram is considered the jewel of the Surya-vamsa, the most upright of all solar kings. Ram is also known as Raghava or Raghupati, after Raghu, one of the most accomplished rulers of the solar dynasty. Raghu was Dashratha's grandfather. Kalidasa in his work, Raghuvamsa, presents his vision of kingship through tales of Raghu's clan.

Raghu was a great warrior. He protected the royal horse enabling his father to perform a hundred yagnas. After he became king, he conquered many lands. His kingdom stretched beyond every horizon. He was therefore acknowledged by all as emperor.

Raghu's son, Aja, was as great a lover as his father was a warrior. Indumati, princess of Vidarbha, chose him as her husband. He loved her so much that when she died, he drowned himself in a river, unable to bear the separation.

But while Raghu establishes dominion over earth and Raghu's son establishes dominion over the heart, Raghu's father demonstrates the behaviour that forms the foundation of kingship.

Dilip

Dilip once did not show the respect due to the divine cow, Kamadhenu, and so was cursed with childlessness. To undo the damage, he swore to serve Kamadhenu's calf, Nandini, for twenty-one days. On the last day of his service, a lion attacked

Nandini. Dilip raised his bow to protect the calf but found he could not move his hands. Dilip begged the lion to spare Nandini. 'What will I eat then?' asked the lion. 'Eat me,' said Dilip. Impressed by this display of commitment and generosity, Nandini revealed that the lion's attack was part of a test. She blessed Dilip that he would be the father of an illustrious son.

Dilip is punished for disrespecting Kamadhenu, the wish-fulfilling cow. Cows in Hindu mythology typically represent the earth. The earth's 'milk' nourishes mankind; in exchange, man, led by kings, is supposed to take care of the earth as a cowherd takes care of a cow. Dilip, though king, disrespects the cow, and hence the earth. He is therefore found so unfit that he is prevented from producing progeny. The curse is lifted only when he learns the true meaning of kingship—to do what animals cannot do: overpower the law of the jungle, and give the weak an opportunity to thrive. While animals are driven by the instinct to survive, humans have the ability to overpower this instinct and make a sacrifice. The more we sacrifice, the less we are driven by self-preservation, the more 'human' we become. Dilip's willingness to die for the cow he has sworn to protect makes him a true king in the eyes of the gods.

At a deeper level, the story of Dilip draws attention to the essential drawback of civilization. Civilization is essentially a manmade construct. It can, and does, interfere with nature. The cow is the lion's natural food and so he has a right over her. It is human intervention that comes in the way. Man's compassion makes no sense to the lion. Thus, a king has to realize that what may seem glorious in the context of civilization may not be so when seen through nature's eyes. Dharma or the code of civilization will constantly be in conflict with our animal urges of sex and violence.

As king, Ram embodies the qualities of Dilip, Raghu and Aja—he has compassion, power and passion. When he wears the crown of his forefathers and sits on the throne of Ayodhya, he strives to establish the perfect kingdom, Ram Rajya, where dharma is upheld by all.

According to Manu, the most perfect society was one where everyone performed their duties determined by their varna or station in society and ashrama or stage in life. This was varna-ashrama-dharma, which sought to create a world that was more organized, predictable and manageable. A king was expected to ensure all his subjects respected this way of life. Ram never questioned varna-ashrama-dharma; he upheld the rules at the cost of personal happiness. That is why he is known as maryada purushottam, the greatest of all kings.

But Ram's determination to uphold varna-ashrama-dharma under all circumstances, without questioning it, presented him with many ethical and moral dilemmas. The choices made by Ram, while being criticized by many, throw light on the inherent tension between manmade laws and natural instincts.

The story of Shambuka from the *Uttara Ramayana*, the final chapter of the *Valmiki Ramayana*, draws attention to the challenge posed to Ram by varna-dharma.

Shambuka

One day a Brahman couple came to Ram's doorstep holding the dead body of their only son. 'Why did my son die before me?' asked the father. 'When the young die before the old, does it not mean that dharma is not being upheld in a kingdom? And when dharma is not upheld, it means the king has failed in his duties. You, Ram, in failing to do your duty as king have caused the death of our son,' said the anguished father. Stung by the accusation, Ram consulted the celestial sage Narada who informed him that a Shudra by the name of Shambuka was performing intense tapasya. As per the code of dharma, only Brahmans were allowed to perform spiritual practices such as tapasya in the first quarter of the world's life cycle, Brahmans and Kshatriyas in the second quarter, Brahmans, Kshatriyas and Vaishyas in the third quarter and Shudras as well in the fourth quarter. As a Shudra, Shambuka was supposed to serve, not perform tapasya, in the Treta yuga to which Ram belonged. By doing so he was violating dharma and this had caused the Brahman's son to die. The only way to make amends was to stop Shambuka's tapasya. Ram hesitated. He asked Shambuka why he was performing tapasya. 'To break free from the cycle of rebirths and attain moksha and be one with God,' said the low-caste man. Ram then raised his sword and beheaded Shambuka. Instantly, Shambuka got what he desired: freedom from the cycle of rebirths and entry into Vishnu's paradise, Vaikunth, as he had been killed by God himself. Further, since dharma had been restored, the Brahman couple's son was restored to life.

At one level, the story of Shambuka can be seen as the reinforcement of caste hierarchy, the crushing of the free will of a man who refuses to submit to rigid codes of conduct imposed by society. At another level it can be seen as the story of a king who has to balance social rules that benefit the community and spiritual aspirations that benefit an individual.

Varna-dharma demanded that everyone fulfil their vocation unquestioningly, vocation being determined by one's lineage. Shambuka breaks his varna-dharma. Ram knows that if Shambuka is allowed to do so, others will follow. This will destabilize society. Hence he reinforces the social structure of his time by beheading Shambuka. As king, he has no choice in this matter. He is supposed to uphold varna-dharma not interpret it.

But at the same time, Ram cannot ignore the spiritual aspiration of Shambuka. Ram faces a conflict between his role as king and his role as God. Must he respect social organization over spiritual aspiration? This conflict, in keeping with the function of mythological tales, is resolved with a possibility grounded in faith. Since Ram is God, his killing of a man leads not to death but to liberation, which is the ultimate goal of all living creatures in the Hindu scheme of things.

It must be noted that the author of the *Ramayana*, Valmiki, was in fact an outcaste bandit called Ratnakar who through the chanting of the name of Ram became a great sage who created the *Ramayana* and ultimately sheltered Sita when she was abandoned by Ram. That Ratnakar does not adhere to the varna-dharma but cleanses himself through meditating on Ram makes it clear that the *Ramayana* and Ram do not dehumanize or devalue people because of their varna.

The varna system of the Vedic period has metamorphosed into jati-pratha or what is called the caste system today. It introduced inhuman practices where, because of one's lineage, people were and still are denied basic human rights like education, water and even the human touch. One has to ask: did Ram subscribe to this? Not according to the *Ramayana* where Ram is shown treating people of all varnas with dignity.

Guha

Ram went deep into the forest and came to a small tribal village. Its chief, Guha, welcomed Ram and offered to let him stay in the village for the entire duration of fourteen years. Ram declined as hermits cannot stay in any settlement. They must

wander and call no place home. Guha organized
a boat to take Ram, Lakshman and Sita cross the
River Ganges. He even washed Ram's feet that had
been soiled by the forest floor. Ram hugged him
with affection and bid him farewell.

For Ram, varna-dharma is a way of organizing society
and determining vocation, not a tool for one group of
people to dominate another. To create hierarchy, to give
value to one group of people over another, would be an
endorsement of the law of the jungle which is against
the spirit of dharma.

That Ram does not dehumanize other varnas is
elaborated in the popular folk story of Shabari. While
Shabari is mentioned in the *Valmiki Ramayana*, her
offering berries to Ram is a later addition that appears
in the Padma Puran traced to around the eleventh
century.

Shabari

While searching for Sita, Ram met residents of the
forests. Amongst them was an old tribal woman
called Shabari. She invited Ram to her house and
offered him some berries. To Lakshman's horror,
Shabari would bite a berry and then either throw it

away or give it to Ram. What surprised Lakshman even more was that Ram would joyfully eat what was offered. Lakshman felt this was a highly insulting way to treat a guest. When he complained, Ram advised him to ask Shabari the reason for her strange behaviour. Shabari replied that she wanted to feed her noble guest the sweetest of berries and the only way to do so was to taste the berries first. What Lakshman saw as insulting behaviour was actually an act of great affection.

Had Ram subscribed to caste excesses, he would never have eaten food from the hands of a tribal woman. That he has no such qualms shows that while Ram, the king, upheld a code of social conduct that determined vocation in his age, he never subscribed either to a code that created hierarchy or to a code that stripped people of their dignity.

While Ram's very own varna-dharma makes him king, his ashrama-dharma makes him husband and householder. These two roles come into conflict when he hears the gossip doing the rounds on the streets of Ayodhya. His subjects feel it is a matter of shame that the queen of the Raghu clan is a woman of soiled reputation, one who spent months in the palace of a lustful demon-king. This presents Ram with his greatest challenge, one that shatters his own personal life.

Abandoning Sita

Ram learnt of a quarrel between a washerman and his wife. The washerman had refused to take his wife back because she had not returned at dusk, as promised, from her mother's house, but at dawn, as she had been delayed by a storm. 'I am not Ram who takes back a wife after she has spent the night in someone else's house,' he said, referring to Sita's stay at Lanka. This comment became the talk of the town. Ram realized that the gossip was harming the reputation of his illustrious household. The people of Ayodhya did not want a woman with a stained reputation as their queen. So he decided to part with his wife. Ram asked Lakshman to take the pregnant Sita out of Ayodhya and leave her in the forest. Abandoned by Ram, all alone in the forest, Sita found shelter in the hermitage of Valmiki, a poet who was composing an epic on the life of Ram which he had heard from the celestial sage, Narada. There she gave birth to her twin sons, Luv and Kush.

Must Ram stand by his faithful wife or must Ram surrender to public opinion to uphold family honour? Must he be husband or king? This story creates a conflict that has no easy answer. It offers no scope for Ram to be both a good king to his people and a good husband to his wife. A choice is demanded and a decision is made.

The decision, however, is highly criticized. How could Ram mistrust Sita despite her trial by fire? How could he give so much value to the words of a washerman?

While the *Valmiki Ramayana* holds gossip responsible for Sita's abandonment from Ram's kingdom, other retellings state that palace intrigues were as much to blame. Jealous of Ram's love for Sita, women in the palace did everything in their power to drive a wedge between the divine couple.

Ravana's drawing

Sita was once asked by the palace women to draw an image of Ravana. Sita who had refused to look upon Ravana's face knew only the shape of his shadow which he cast on the earth and the sea while taking her across to Lanka in his flying chariot. After much persuasion, she agreed to trace it out on the wall. Later when she was away, the same palace women showed Ram the image drawn by Sita on the wall. 'She still thinks of him,' they said poisoning Ram's mind against his innocent wife.

Folk narratives from Kerala say that the women responsible for doing so were actually disguised Rakshasa women, the wives and sisters of Ravana determined to avenge his defeat.

Throughout the *Ramayana*, Ram is always projected as king, not husband. He is always rather aloof with Sita, treating her with almost ritual propriety, never displaying his passion for her, for passion is considered unsuitable for a king, the root of many ills. After all it was passion for Kaikeyi that led Dashratha to give the two boons that caused Ram's exile in the first place. The only time Ram publicly demonstrates his deep love for Sita is when he first learns of Sita's abduction by Ravana. He mourns his loss as a lovebird mourns the passing away of its beloved. He loses his poise and submits to the pain of separation, an act that is seen by Lakshman as indulgence for a king, and therefore highly inappropriate.

Ram's grief

Having discovered that the golden deer was actually a demon, Ram realized this was an elaborate decoy to draw him away from the grass hut. As he rushed back, he saw Lakshman running towards him. Both realized that they had been tricked by Rakshasas. They rushed back to the grass hut where their worst fear was realized—Sita had disappeared. There was some sign of struggle but no footprints. A nervous and agitated Ram begged the trees and the animals in the vicinity to tell him where his Sita was. They scoured the forest around the hut and found the vulture, Jatayu, lying on the forest floor bleeding to death. 'Ravana, king of Rakshasas, has taken Sita on his flying chariot and gone south. I tried my best to stop him but failed. Forgive me, Ram,' Jatayu said and then breathed his last. Ram's heart sank when he heard this. Sita, daughter of a king, daughter-in-law of a king, had abandoned the pleasures of the palace and followed him to the forest and endured the harsh conditions stoically. She was his responsibility and he had failed her. He felt her helplessness and terror at being touched by a brute. He wept. Lakshman comforted his brother and then admonished him for displaying such emotions. 'It is unbecoming of a scion of the solar clan to behave so,' he said.

Ram, the husband, is never allowed to grieve by Ram, the king. He is not allowed to wallow in self-pity. He is expected to rescue Sita, not out of love for his wife, but because it is his duty as king.

When Ravana is killed, Ram does not rush to meet Sita. Instead he treats her with a formality that almost borders on cruelty. He first crowns Vibhishana king and only then sends for her. When she arrives full of expectation, he says he rescued her because it was his duty to wipe out the stain on his family's honour. Thus shame, not love, is what brought him to Lanka. He insists that Sita prove to the world that she has indeed been faithful despite spending months in Ravana's palace.

A perfect king is not allowed to be emotional. Everything has to be correct, formal, public. Ram's relationship with Sita is always aimed at pleasing society. There is nothing private or personal about it. And so when people complain that their queen is stained by reputation, the scion of the solar dynasty is forced to abandon Sita, who though innocent in person has become the symbol of royal shame.

Later, Ram is asked to perform the Ashwamedha yagna. To perform this ritual he needs a wife by his side. In Sita's absence, the people ask Ram to take another wife. His father after all had three wives. But Ram refuses to do so: he has given up the queen his people did not want but he had never given up his wife. Thus by refusing to take another wife he endorses his position as ekam-patni-vrata, faithful to a single wife, the only character in Hindu chronicles to be recognized so.

Golden Sita

Ram decided to perform the Ashwamedha yagna as part of which the royal horse would travel around the world followed by Ram's army. All the lands it traversed unchallenged would come under Ram's suzerainty. Those who stopped the horse would have to face the might of Ram's soldiers. No king could perform this ritual without a wife by his side. Since Sita was no longer in Ayodhya by Ram's side, the sages advised Ram to marry again. Ram refused to do so. Instead he placed next to him an image of Sita made of gold.

That Ram uses gold to make the image of Sita is significant. Gold is the purest of metals that can never be contaminated or corrupted. Thus, symbolically, Ram,

Devdutt Pattanaik

the husband, projects to his people his own opinion of his wife. He does not doubt her chastity.

To stretch the point further—is it justice for a husband to abandon a woman on grounds of adultery? As an epic, the *Ramayana* celebrates compassion not righteous indignation. It repeatedly forgives human frailties. One must never forget that the unfaithful Ahalya, who was cruelly turned to stone by her husband, is liberated by none other than Ram. This situation of Ram abandoning Sita has nothing to do with the issue of adultery; it has everything to do with the issue of governance. Should governance be determined by a king's will or by public opinion or should both, people and king, be governed by an impersonal dharma? And is Ram husband first or king?

In Indian literature, the separation of lovers is a popular theme for plays and songs. The separation of Ram and Sita because of social issues is no exception. In the forest, Sita single-handedly raises her twin sons. They grow up to be fine singers whose songs stir the soul and ask heart-wrenching questions on the validity of social values.

Luv and Kush

As Ram performed the Ashwamedha yagna, news reached him that two boys, twins, were going around the city, lute in hand, singing a song composed by Valmiki. They were narrating the story of Ram—his great fourteen-year forest adventure. At the end of the narration, which concluded with the defeat of Ravana and the coronation of Ram, the children were called to the palace and given gifts by Ram, who did not recognize his own sons. The boys were very pleased to see Ram but they did not find Sita beside him. 'Where is she?' they asked innocently. 'In the forest,' replied Ram. 'Why? What did she do wrong?' asked the children. Ram had no answer.

Ram's children are symbols of Ram's marriage. Besides challenging Ram's decision to abandon Sita, they also challenge his authority by confronting his army, the symbol of his kingship.

Victory over Ram's army

Luv and Kush caught hold of Ram's horse and thereby challenged Ram's authority. Ram's soldiers who followed the royal horse tried to make the children see sense but the twins refused to part with the horse. Finally the soldiers decided to use force. They raised their weapons. To their astonishment, the two boys turned out to be fierce warriors. They too raised their weapons and fought with such skill that the soldiers were forced to retreat. Luv and Kush were able to defeat Ram's entire army including his brothers, Lakshman, Bharata and Shatrughna. They were even able to imprison Hanuman. Finally Ram was forced to join the fight. But even he was no match for the children. The people of Ayodhya realized that the twins were no ordinary children. When Valmiki came into the battlefield and revealed that the two boys were the sons of Sita, it was clear to all that dharma stood not with Ram or Ayodhya but with Sita and her children for victory always follows righteousness.

Ram who could defeat Ravana with an army of monkeys is unable to defeat the sons of Sita with an army of powerful soldiers. It is the only defeat that Ram faces in his entire life. According to Hindu belief, victory always sides with those who uphold dharma. Ram's defeat by Sita's sons thus implies Sita's moral high ground over Ram. In Ram's defeat, the imbalance created by his unfair decision to abandon Sita is rectified.

The Ayodhya that gossiped about Sita's character and forced its king to abandon his queen upholds dharma only in word, not in spirit. It did not see Sita's heart; it saw only her reputation. This loss of moral authority results in the defeat of Ayodhya's mighty army by two children. A humiliated Ayodhya realizes its mistake and begs Sita to return. Ram, the husband, is most pleased. Ram, the king, then requests Sita to display her chastity publicly once again, so that no one questions his honour ever again.

Sita returns to earth

'Do it once more. Then, you had done it before monkeys and demons. Now, do it before my people,' said Ram. Tired of her morality being put on public display repeatedly, Sita decided to take a drastic step. She joined her palms and said, 'If I have been true to Ram may the earth split open and take me into its bosom.' Instantly the earth split open and Sita slipped into the ground. Ram watched his beloved disappear under the earth right before his eyes. He tried to stop her but he could catch hold of just one strand of Sita's hair. This turned into the sacred grass known as kusha.

With Sita gone, Ram, the husband, loses all interest in worldly life. But Ram, the king, continues to do his royal duty until death comes to him and tells him it is time to die.

Ram enters the Sarayu

After Sita was swallowed by the earth, Ram performed his kingly duties until finally he was informed by the gods that the time had come for him to leave the earth and return to Vaikunth. He divided his kingdom amongst his sons and then walked into the Sarayu river to discard his mortal flesh.

Like Shambuka's beheading, the story of Sita's abandonment is edited out of most retellings and translations. Both make uncomfortable reading. Both challenge Ram's uprightness. But it is precisely these incidents that show what makes Ram divine.

Mythological stories are meant to resolve insurmountable emotional and social conflicts through events that are grounded in faith, and are hence by nature fantastic not realistic. In Shambuka's story, his beheading by God, and not a mortal king, restores social organization (different roles of different varnas in different yugas) while respecting the essential equality of all souls (eternal desire of every living creature for moksha). In Sita's story, the implausible defeat of Ram's army by his two sons, resolves the conflict between Ram's role as king (law) and Ram's trust in his wife (justice).

At all times, Ram remains upright, faithful to dharma alone, motivated not by authority but by the larger good, struggling to harmonize apparently irreconcilable forces, driven not by passion but by duty, not by power for the self but by love for others. That is what makes Ram the model king.

9

Vishnu's Incarnation

I am grateful to you
Lord of the universe
For touching me with the dust of your feet
Dust that all the gods long for
It is strange, Ram
How you enchant everyone
Behaving as human do
Bringing happiness everywhere
Without walking anywhere

—From the prayer of Ahalya in *Adhyatma Ramayana*

God on earth

Hindus believe that God is both nirguna, without form, and saguna, with form. God with form has multiple manifestations as no single form can convey the notion of completeness. Traditionally, the male trinity of Brahma, Vishnu or Shiva along with the female trinity of Saraswati, Lakshmi and Shakti embody God.

Brahma, in the form of a passionate priest, opens his eyes to desire and creates the world. Shiva, in the form of an indifferent ascetic, shuts his eyes to desire and destroys the world. Vishnu stands in between them, as the sustainer, balancing desire with detachment, ensuring there is order and stability in the world. The world that thus created, sustained and destroyed is the source of all knowledge, wisdom and power embodied in Saraswati, Lakshmi and Shakti.

Vishnu institutes and maintains order in the universe through the code of dharma. With the passage of time, this code gets corrupted. At regular intervals Vishnu descends from his paradise, Vaikunth, to redefine dharma for a particular era or yuga. These descents of Vishnu are his avatars or incarnations.

Hindus believe that the world goes through cycles of rebirth like all living creatures. The world's life cycle can be broken down into four eras — Krita, Treta, Dvapar and Kali. Vishnu descends when one yuga is giving way to the next. He was Parashuram at the end of the Krita yuga, the first quarter. He was Ram at the end of the Treta yuga. He was Krishna at the end of the Dvapar yuga. And he will be Kalki at the end of the Kali yuga.

But it is not divine duty alone that makes Vishnu incarnate on earth. The Bhagavat Puran informs us that Vishnu descends not just to save mankind but also to liberate his doorkeepers from a curse.

Jaya and Vijaya

The two doorkeepers of Vaikunth would not let the four boy-sages, the Sanat Kumars, enter because Vishnu was asleep. Enraged at being kept away from God, the four Kumars cursed the doorkeepers that they would lose their exalted position so close to God and be born away from him on earth as two Rakshasa brothers—Ravana and Kumbhakarna. On learning that his doorkeepers had been cursed for doing their duty, Vishnu declared that he would himself descend on earth as Ram and to release his doorkeepers from their demonic form. No sooner were the two doorkeepers born on earth as Rakshasas than they began living a life with total disregard for dharma, in the hope that Vishnu would relieve them of their demonic life sooner rather than later.

Another story informs us that Vishnu descended as Parashuram, Ram and Krishna to kill the greedy rulers of the earth after the earth goddess complained that she could not bear their weight any more. According to the Padma Puran, Vishnu himself is compelled by a curse to live on earth as Parashuram, Ram and Krishna, making God very much a part of the web of karma that makes the Hindu world go round.

Beheading Kavyamata

Once while Shukra was away performing a penance, the Devas decided to attack and kill the Asuras. Without their guru, the Asuras were helpless so they sought the help of Kavyamata,

Shukra's mother. She assured them of her support. She decided to cast a spell that would put all the Devas to sleep. As she was about to chant the magical mantra to make this happen, Vishnu hurled his discus and severed her neck. When Shukra learnt of this he accused Vishnu of stri-hatya-paap, the crime of killing a woman. 'Only when you live as a mortal for three lifetimes will you be cleansed of this crime,' said Shukra and so Vishnu was born on earth as Parashuram, Ram and Krishna.

Although Parashuram, Ram and Krishna live in different ages and are involved in different crises, their tales are not independent of each other. There are deep connections between apparently disparate events in their lives thus driving home the point that all three of them are merely part of a much grander design. The story of Parashuram, for example, is curiously similar to that of Vasishtha and Vishwamitra found in the *Ramayana*.

Parashuram annihilates the warriors

King Kartaviryarjun coveted the wish-fulfilling divine cow called Kamadhenu that was in the possession of Rishi Jamadagni. When he tried to take the cow by force, he was stopped by Jamadagni's youngest son, Parashuram, who hacked the king to death with an axe. In retaliation, the king's sons killed Jamadagni. An enraged Parashuram, went about killing all the sons of the king and all their descendants and all their allies. He killed so many warriors that he filled five great lakes with their blood.

Parashuram kills the king who steals his father's cow. Ram, on the other hand, accepts as his teacher Vishwamitra who as Kaushik had stolen Vasishtha's cow. This clearly indicates a shift in values from Krita yuga to Treta yuga.

This shift in values is evident even in the way Parashuram and Ram deal with adultery. Parashuram beheads his mother, Renuka, for momentarily desiring a man who is not her husband. Ram, on the other hand, liberates Ahalya who is turned to stone by her husband when he finds her in the arms of Indra. In the Treta yuga, Vishnu seems to be making more room for human frailty.

When Ram breaks Shiva's bow to win Sita's hand in marriage, he is challenged by Parashuram himself to string the bow of Vishnu. When Ram succeeds, Parashuram realizes his time is over. The young lad before him is, like him, Vishnu's incarnation, but one who is more appropriate for the Treta yuga.

Just as the Treta yuga is less perfect than the Krita yuga, the Dvapar yuga is even more imperfect than the Treta yuga. A new avatar of Vishnu is needed for this era—not Ram, but Krishna.

Ram is maryada purushottam, the supreme keeper of rules, while Krishna is leela purushottam, the best game player. Both stand for dharma, but their approach is different. For Ram, the means is as important as the end; for Krishna only the end matters and the spirit of the law is more important than the letter of the law. That is why perhaps, only Ram is visualized as king while Krishna remains a kingmaker. Unlike Ram who is faithful to only one wife, Krishna loves many women, each with the same intensity. The reason for this is karma says one folk story.

When I become Krishna

As Ram passed through a forest looking for Sita, the trees, the birds, the animals and the sages of the forest were drawn to his beauty and august presence. 'Come to us. Let us comfort you,' they said. 'No,' said Ram, 'none but Sita shall comfort me in this life. I am hers alone.' Then, looking at their unhappy faces he assured them that in his next life when he would be Krishna, all of them would be reborn as milkmaids in Vrindavan. Together they would dance in the meadows of Madhuvan all through autumn nights. For as Krishna, he would be able to love more than one.

According to another folk retelling, Ram asked Manthara to poison Kaikeyi's mind. 'Only then will I be able to go to the forest and kill Ravana,' Ram explained. With a heavy heart, Manthara obeyed God. Pleased with her devotion he said, 'In your next life you will be as hunchbacked as you are now. But while you cause Ram misery, Krishna will embrace you and bring you much joy.' And so the Bhagavat Puran informs us that when Krishna entered Mathura he embraced a hunchbacked maid called Kubja or Trivakra with such passion that her back straightened and she became a beautiful woman. This Kubja was none other than Manthara reborn.

Ram and Krishna are linked to each other through Hanuman also. While Ram is said to have ridden on Hanuman's shoulders in battle in the *Ramayana*,

Hanuman resides in the flag atop Arjuna's war chariot that is driven by Krishna in the *Mahabharata*.

Ram and Krishna are also connected to each other through Jambavan, the king of the bears, who joined Ram's monkey army to rescue Sita. His daughter, Jambavati, becomes one of Krishna's chief queens.

It is said that as Krishna, Vishnu balances the imbalances created by Ram. Ram created an imbalance by killing Vali, son of Indra, by shooting him in the back while he was engaged in a duel with Sugriva, son of Surya. To balance the score, when Vishnu descended as Krishna, he had Arjuna, son of Kunti by Indra, shoot and kill Karna, son of Kunti by Surya, while the latter had his back turned and was busy pulling out his chariot wheel that had got stuck in the ground.

When the tales of Parashuram, Ram and Krishna are compared with each other, we find that they reflect the different responses of Vishnu to social and spiritual values that are eroding with the march of time.

The three incarnations of Vishnu are very different from each other in character and behaviour. Parashuram is an outraged priest; Ram is a straightforward warrior; Krishna is a charismatic, charming and shrewd strategist. Parashuram ruthlessly punishes those who fail to uphold dharma, sparing neither king nor mother. Ram acts with more empathy but gives utmost importance to the law. Krishna bends and breaks the rules when they lack the spirit of dharma.

Parashuram is born a Brahman but is always visualized as a warrior carrying a bow and an axe. Krishna is born a Kshatriya but is always visualized as a cowherd or charioteer. Only Ram is born a Kshatriya and is visualized performing his caste role, as king and warrior.

In each incarnation, Vishnu is accompanied by Lakshmi, his consort. While he protects her each time, her relationship with him differs with each incarnation. For Parashuram, Lakshmi is his mother, Renuka, and his cow, Kamadhenu, who must be protected from the lustful and greedy Kshatriyas. For Ram, Lakshmi is Sita, the faithful and domesticated wife, who has to be rescued from the Rakshasas. For Krishna, Lakshmi is Draupadi, who he has to rescue because Draupadi's own husbands, instead of taking care of her, gamble her away and allow her to be disrobed in public.

With each incarnation, Lakshmi's situation worsens as she drifts away from Vishnu. Each time, Vishnu manages to rescue her, as son, husband or friend, and restore dharma. But a time will come when things will be beyond repair. Then Vishnu will descend as Kalki and destroy the world himself. This will happen at the end of Kali yuga, after which the world will die, an event known as pralay or dissolution. After pralay, a new world will be born. A new kalpa with four new yugas. As time marches ahead, Vishnu will descend once more as Ram in the Treta yuga, after Parashuram of the Krita yuga but before Krishna of the Dvapar yuga.

Ram and the *Ramayana* thus cannot be seen in isolation. To fully appreciate Ram, his saga has to be compared and contrasted with the stories of Parashuram and Krishna that are partly told in the *Mahabharata* and partly in the Bhagavat Puran. All these have to be seen as part of the Vishnu Puran or the lore of Vishnu. To better understand the Vishnu Puran, one has to compare it with the lore of Shiva and Brahma, the Shiva Puran and the Brahma Puran. These make sense only when compared with the Devi Puran, the lore of Saraswati, Lakshmi and Shakti. All these tales are grounded in the wisdom of the Vedas, making Ram one piece of the grand Hindu jigsaw puzzle.

10

Valmiki's Inspiration

Sweeter than sugar, tastier than curd,
Sweeter indeed than honey is the name of Ram
Constant repetition of this sweet name
Gives one the taste of divine nectar
Therefore, chant the name of Ram constantly

— A Telugu prayer

Many retellings, single tradition

Tradition has it that the goddess Shakti once asked Shiva what will give man hope in the Kali yuga, the spiritually bereft final quarter of the world's life cycle. Shiva replied that hope would come from the hearing of Ram's tale. Narada heard Shiva narrate the whole story to the goddess. He in turn passed it on to a highway robber called Ratnakar, who later in life became known as Valmiki.

Ratnakar

A highway robber called Ratnakar once attacked Narada with the intention of stealing his lute. 'Please, before you strike me, tell me why are you doing this?' Narada asked, as Ratnakar was about to kill him. 'I have no other means to feed my family,' Ratnakar replied. 'So you are doing this for your family. Does that mean they will share the burden of this crime?' Narada inquired. 'Yes, of course,' said Ratnakar. 'Are you sure?' Narada persisted, making Ratnakar suddenly unsure. 'Why don't you confirm this with them?' Narada suggested. So Ratnakar tied Narada to a tree and went home and asked his wife and son if they would share the burden of his crime. 'Why should we?' asked his wife. 'It is your duty to feed us. What you do for that is solely your responsibility.' Ratnakar realized at that moment that ultimately one is responsible for all of one's actions; one cannot blame others for it. He returned to Narada a changed man. 'How do I cleanse myself of this burden of crime?' he asked. 'Chant Ram's name,' said Narada. But Ratnakar was such a terrible criminal that Ram's name could not even form on his tongue. Narada then said, 'Chant maramara repeatedly.' Mara means 'die'. Being a killer, Ratnakar could utter the word easily. 'Mara-mara-mara . . . die-die-die . . . ' Slowly the sound changed, 'Ma-ra-ma-ra-ma-ra-ma-Ram-Ram-Ram.' Thus the word meaning death reversed itself to become the name of God who liberates one from death. So

Devdutt Pattanaik

intense was Ratnakar's chanting that he lost all sense of the world. When he finally awoke from his meditative trance he found he was covered by a termite hill made of sand or valu. As a result Ratnakar came to be known as Valmiki. Valmiki then learnt from Narada the story of Ram and he took it upon himself to turn this story into a song that would inspire all of humanity.

A pair of parrots heard Valmiki's composition. According to the Padma Puran, the parrots narrated this tale to Sita before her marriage. But they did not know the whole tale. Angry, Sita locked them up in a cage and one of the parrots died. The survivor cursed Sita that she too would experience separation from her husband. And that is why Sita was abandoned by Ram soon after their return to Ayodhya.

How could Sita hear the *Ramayana* when she played a role in it? The explanation given is that the *Ramayana* that was narrated by Shiva, then Narada, then Valmiki and finally the parrot was the *Satakoti Ramacharitra* or the timeless *Ramayana*, which becomes reality in every Treta yuga, the second quarter of the world's life cycle. In traditional Hindu thought, the *Ramayana* is an eternal story, not the creation of one poet, not restricted to one period. Thus the *Valmiki Ramayana* is not the 'original' *Ramayana*. It is simply the oldest known *Ramayana* retold by a sage called Valmiki.

Valmiki's *Ramayana* is generally treated as Adi Kavya, the first Sanskrit poetry ever written. While it was part of oral tradition for centuries, it reached its final form somewhere between 200 BCE (Before Common Era, formerly known as BC) and 200 CE (Common Era, formerly known as AD). The content took a lyrical form after Valmiki experienced a painful episode.

From pain comes poetry

Valmiki once saw a hunter shoot down one of a pair of lovebirds. The surviving bird flew around in circles over the corpse of its beloved, wailing and moaning and finally dying of heartbreak. Pained by this sight, Valmiki cursed the hunter for his crime. The curse came in the form of a verse and Valmiki realized that the roots of poetry lay in pain. As he witnessed the pain of Sita's life, who took shelter in his hermitage after she was cast away by Ram for no fault of hers, he was inspired to compose the epic of *Ramayana*. He taught it to Sita's twin sons. So sweet was their rendition of this song that they were invited to sing before Ram himself in Ayodhya. They did not know that the man before them was their father. And Ram did not know that the young children singing his song were his own two sons.

The Ramayana also happens to be part of the *Mahabharata*, dated between 300 BCE and 300 CE, where it is called the Ramopakhyan. When the Pandavas bemoaned their thirteen years of forest exile, Rishi Markandeya retorted by telling them how Ram suffered for fourteen years and while the Pandavas deserved their punishment for gambling away their kingdom, Ram did not deserve his fate—he was simply obeying his father.

Though Buddhists and Jains turned away from mainstream Hinduism, they could not turn away from Ram.

The Buddhist *Dashratha Jatak*, written in Prakrit and dated to around 300 CE, identifies Ram as a Bodhisattva, or Buddha in an earlier life. Ram of the Buddhists is portrayed as a man full of integrity, compassion and wisdom who is fully aware that all things in this world, from kings to kingdoms, are impermanent.

Jains too had great regard for Ram. In the many Jain *Ramayana*s known as *Puama-cariya* or *Padma Charitra*, first written in Apabhramsha in 300 CE by Vimalasuri, and then adapted by many authors right up to 1600 CE, Ram, also known as Padma, displays all Jain virtues. Thus, the Jain Ram is too noble to be violent. As an upholder of Jain ideals, he does not kill Ravana. That task is left to the more aggressive Lakshman.

The great poet Kalidasa wrote the *Raghuvamsa*, the story of Ram's ancestors in the fifth century CE. The playwright Bhavabhuti wrote *Mahaviracharitra* and *Uttaramacharitra* in the eighth century AD based on the early and later life of Ram. All these works were written in classical Sanskrit.

From the twelfth century onwards, as many of India's local languages took shape, poets started writing the *Ramayana* in tongues that reached out to larger audiences. The *Ramayana* was amongst the first pieces of literature in most regional languages. Some of the more popular regional retellings of this sacred epic are:

- Tamil *Ramayana* by Kamban in the twelfth century
- Telugu *Ranganatha Ramayana* by Buddha Reddy in the thirteenth century
- Assamese *Kotha Ramayana* by Madhava Kandali in the fourteenth century

- Oriya *Dandi Ramayana* by Balaram Das in the fifteenth century
- Kannada *Torave Ramayana* by Narahari in the fifteenth century
- Bengali *Ramayana* by Krittivasa in the fifteenth century
- Malayalam *Adhyatma Ramayana* by Ezhuthachan in the sixteenth century
- Hindi *Ram-charit-manas* by Goswami Tulsidas in the sixteenth century
- Marathi *Bhavarth Ramayana* by Ekanath in the sixteenth century
- Punjabi *Govind Ramayana* by Guru Gobind Singh, the tenth guru of the Sikh community, in the seventeenth century
- Kashmiri *Ramayana* by Divakar Prakash Bhat in the eighteenth century
- Gujarati *Giridhar Ramayana* by Giridharadas in the nineteen century

Each *Ramayana* gives the audience something new to think about, a new insight into Ram's tale which is actually a new insight about their own life. That is what has made the story of Ram come alive and remain relevant through the ages.

In the *Adbhut Ramayana*, Sita is even presented as daughter of Ravana's chief queen, Mandodari, giving a new twist to the tale.

Mandodari's daughter

Ravana, king of Rakshasas, used to harass Rishis. He would even charge them a tax. And if they could not pay the tax, he would take their blood and collect it in a pot, intent on using their spiritually endowed fluid for an occult ritual that would make him even more powerful. Ravana's wife, Mandodari, unaware of what her husband was up to, wondered what was in the pot he kept so securely in his chambers. One day, unable to restrain herself, she picked up the pot and took a sip of the fluid inside. Instantly she became pregnant and delivered a girl child. A heavenly voice boomed that this girl would be the killer of her father. Fearing for Ravana, at the same time not wanting to harm her newborn daughter, Mandodari put the baby in a box and set it afloat on the sea. The sea god gave the girl to the earth goddess who gave her to Janaka, who adopted her and named her Sita.

In Kamban's Tamil retelling, a minor twist in the tale adds greater emotional intensity to the episode of Dashratha's death.

Last rites by Shatrughna

Shortly after Ram left for the forest, Dashratha died of a broken heart. It was a tragic moment; despite having four sons, not one was by his side when he died. Two had been exiled to the forest. The other two had gone to visit their maternal uncle. When Bharata and Shatrughna returned to Ayodhya, they were shattered by the sight of their father's corpse embalmed in a vat of medicated oil. Bharata, being the eldest son present there, was expected to perform the funeral rites. But Vasishtha informed him that before dying, Dashratha had expressly instructed that Kaikeyi's son should not be allowed to cremate him. Thus it was left to the youngest son, Shatrughna, to cremate Dashratha.

Krittivasa's Bengali *Ramayana* is amongst the earliest retellings to introduce us to the Lakshman rekha, the line that Sita was not supposed to cross. Valmiki makes no mention of this line yet today it forms an integral part of any *Ramayana* narration. Likewise, the story of Shabari feeding berries to Ram comes not from the *Valmiki Ramayana* but from the eleventh century Padma Puran.

Perhaps uncomfortable with the idea of Sita being touched by a demon, some retellings like the *Adhyatma Ramayana* in Malayalam suggest that the Sita who Ravana abducted was not Sita but a double. This narrative introduces us to another character, Vedavati, who is now part of Ram's folklore.

Maya Sita

The Sita that Ravana abducted was not the real Sita. While Ram and Lakshman were away chasing the golden deer, a duplicate of Sita had emerged from the kitchen fire of Sita's grass hut. She identified herself as Vedavati, a hermit woman whom Ravana had once tried to rape. To save herself, she had jumped into fire and sworn that she would be the cause of Ravana's death. Vedavati told Sita of what was to pass and advised her to enter the fire and live with Agni, the fire god, until the death of Ravana while she took her place. Sita did as advised and Ravana ended up abducting Vedavati assuming she was Sita. After Ravana was killed and Ram asked his wife to prove her chastity by

Devdutt Pattanaik

walking through fire, the duplicate Sita walked into the fire while the real Sita walked out. For helping Sita, Vedavati was given a boon that in Kali yuga she would marry Vishnu.

Nature has always played an important role in most *Ramayana* retellings. The *Bhil Ramayana*, also known as *Rom Sitma ni Varta*, informs us that Sita had six fingers. She cut the sixth finger from which rose the bamboo tree. From the Oriya *Ramayana* of Balaram Das comes the now-popular children's story of how squirrels came to have a striped back.

Squirrel's stripes

While the bridge to Lanka was being built, Ram noticed a tiny squirrel carrying a tiny pebble towards the sea, determined to play his part in rescuing Sita. While the monkeys were amused by this, Ram was so moved that he caressed the back of the squirrel. This left a mark on the squirrel's back. Since that day all squirrels have stripes on their back, a reminder of Ram's grateful touch.

Indian traders took the *Ramayana* to Southeast Asia and the story of Ram is now an integral part of

Indonesian, Thai and Malay cultures inspiring theatre, shadow puppetry and brilliant mural paintings.

The *Ramayana* in Thailand, written by the kings of Siam, is called *Ramakirti* or *Ramakien*. It narrates the tale of Phra Ram who is king of Ayutthaya, and the avatar of Phra Narai (the Thai Vishnu). Here, Hanuman plays an important role. But this Hanuman is not the devoted celibate servant that Hindus of India are familiar with; he is a romantic adventurer who helps Ram defeat Tosakan, the Thai Ravana. The following story illustrates how Thai kings portrayed Hanuman as the very capable monkey-general of Ram.

Hanuman's tail

A mermaid queen kept destroying the bridge to Lanka on Ravana's instructions until Hanuman went underwater and overpowered her. When the bridge was finally built and the monkeys began to cross it, Ravana shot two powerful arrows and broke the two ends of the bridge, trapping Ram and his army in the middle. Hanuman then increased his size to that of a giant, and used his tail to bridge the gap. Ram and his army then crossed over to Lanka on Hanuman's mighty tail.

In the war between the Rakshasas and the Vanaras, many new characters were created in many Ram-kathas to spice up the action. One of them was Mahiravana, sometimes known as Ahiravana, a sorcerer who lived in the nether regions. This character, also found in the Sanskrit Agni Puran, is believed to have been inspired by the rise of Tantra and black magic in medieval times especially in the eastern parts of India.

Mahiravana

On his brother's request, the sorcerer Mahiravana put all the monkeys to sleep and carried Ram and Lakshman to his subterranean lair with the intention of sacrificing them to the goddess Kali so as to get more occult powers. Hanuman managed to track Mahiravana's path and, in the form of a bee, he entered the sorcerer's lair. 'When he is ready to make the sacrifice, he will ask you to bow your head and place it on the chopping block,' said Hanuman to Ram. 'Tell him then that being the son of a king you do not know how to bow your head. Ask him to demonstrate.' Ram did as Hanuman advised. An exasperated Mahiravana agreed to demonstrate. He bowed his head and placed it on the chopping block. In a flash, Hanuman swung the sacrificial sword and severed Mahiravana's neck. The promised offering was made to Kali. But it was not Ram's head that she was given. It was Mahiravana's.

As the worship of the goddess became widespread, many tales emerged that portrayed Sita not as a victim but as the real power behind Ram who chose to appear demure so that her husband could take the credit of victory. The following story is found in the *Adbhut Ramayana*.

Thousand-headed Ravana

Ayodhya was once attacked by the son of Ravana. While his father had only ten heads, he had a thousand heads and was thus more powerful. All of Ram's army tried to destroy this Rakshasa but failed. Ram and his brothers tried to kill him but were no match for him. Finally, they realized that only the power of a chaste woman could kill him. They called all the women of Ayodhya to fight the demon but none had the power to stop him. Finally, Sita was summoned. Sita transformed into Kali, with a thousand heads, and as many arms and feet, her head reaching beyond the skies, fire pouring out of her mouth. She killed the apparently invincible thousand-headed demon in an instant. The sight of Sita as Kali terrified Ram. He sang songs to her glory and begged her to return to her earthly form.

The twentieth century saw Ram on celluloid with films like *Bharata Milap* (1942), *Ram Rajya* (1943) and *Sati Sulochana* (1961). Ramanand Sagar's television serial *Ramayana*, with Arun Govil starring as Ram, made history in the late 1980s. All of India came to a standstill when it was telecast every Sunday morning for over a year. While he used the *Tulsi Ramayana* as the primary source of inspiration, he did try to incorporate other *Ramayana*s into the storyline. The celluloid Ram has created lasting visual impressions: Ram today cannot be visualized with a moustache and for many children, Sita wore the sari in Gujarati style while she was in the forest. Like the *Tulsi Ramayana*, Sagar's *Ramayana* ends with the coronation of Ram in Ayodhya, a happy ending that makes for family viewing. The *Uttar Ramayana* was treated as a separate serial.

The twenty-first century has witnessed several other recreations of the story of the *Ramayana*. In 2006 Virgin Comics brought out *Ramayana* 3392 AD, a brainchild of Deepak Chopra and Shekhar Kapur. It features a reimagining of the epic in a post-apocalyptic future where Ram leads the last of the human kingdoms against the demon-lord Ravana.

By the looks of it Ram's story will continue to be written in the years to come. But all authors must always keep in mind why the *Ramayana* is to be written.

Hanuman Nataka

Valmiki heard that Hanuman had written a *Ramayana*. So he travelled north to the plantain grove where Hanuman resided. There, etched on the rocks, he found Hanuman's *Ramayana*. It was the most brilliant piece of literature that Valmiki had ever read. Tears rolled down Valmiki's cheeks. 'Why do you cry?' asked Hanuman. 'Because your work is so beautiful,' said Valmiki, 'and because after reading your work no one will read mine.' Hanuman felt sorry for Valmiki and without any qualms, with a flick of his tail, smashed all the rocks that had Ram's tale etched on them. 'Stop! What are you doing?' asked Valmiki. 'Making you happy,' replied Hanuman. 'I wrote the *Ramayana* only to remember Ram. But you seem to have written the *Ramayana* so that you will be remembered.' A much-humbled Valmiki realized then that while he had written the tale of Ram, he had not absorbed the spirit of Ram's life as Hanuman had.

The *Ramayana* has never been a tale of Ram's life. It is a tale of how Ram lived for others. By retelling his tale, storytellers hope to inspire themselves and others to live as Ram did.

11

Hindutva's Icon

Why would anyone want to learn anything
But Ram?
From the grass to the ant
Everything that lived,
Everything that moved,
Everything that stood motionless
He raised everything
To the highest of states

—Tamil song by the ninth-century poet-saint
Nammalvar

Politics of the soul

Is Ram real? For Hindus, he is.

All across India are sites associated with Ram's life—Ayodhya in Uttar Pradesh where he was born, Chitrakut, also in Uttar Pradesh, where he stayed in the early days of his forest exile, Panchavati in Maharashtra from where Sita was abducted, Hampi where Ram met Hanuman, Rameshwaram in Tamil Nadu from where he built a bridge to Lanka, and Rishikesh where he performed penance to atone for the crime of killing Ravana who though demon, was also a Brahman by birth. The days of Ram's birth, of his victory over Ravana and of his return to Ayodhya are known and celebrated as Ram Navami, Dusshera and Diwali festivals. Even Ram's horoscope is known to astrologers; it shows all the signs of him being a great man.

Does this make Ram a historical figure? Yes, for Hindus it does. But the Hindu notion of history is quite different from the popular notion of history as the following episode from a folk Ram-katha informs us.

Ram's ring

Ram was informed that it was time for him to die but that Yama, god of death, could not reach him because he was afraid of Hanuman who guarded the gates of Ram's palace. To allow Yama's entry, it was necessary to distract Hanuman. So Ram dropped his ring into a crack in the palace floor and requested Hanuman to fetch it. Hanuman reduced himself to the size of a beetle and entered the crack only to discover that it was no crack but the entrance to a tunnel that led to Naga-lok, the land of serpents. Hanuman met Vasuki, king of serpents, and informed him of his mission. 'Go to the ring room. There are many rings there. Maybe you will find the one that belongs to Ram,' said Vasuki. Sure enough, Hanuman found Ram's ring there. But to his astonishment, all the rings in the room, and there were hundreds of them, were copies of Ram's ring. 'What is the meaning of this?' he asked bewildered. Vasuki smiled and said, 'This world we live in goes through cycles of life and death. Each life cycle of the world is called a kalpa. Each kalpa is composed of four yugas or quarters. In the second quarter or Treta yuga, Ram takes birth in Ayodhya. Then one day his ring falls from earth into the subterranean realm of serpents through a tunnel. A monkey follows it and Ram up there dies. So it has been for hundreds of thousands of kalpas. All these rings testify to that fact. And look there are empty rooms in Naga-lok waiting for the rings of the future Rams.' Hanuman realized that this was Ram's way of telling him that he could not stop death from coming. Ram would die. The world would die. But like all things Ram would be reborn each time the world is reborn. So it would be forever.

This cyclical notion of history makes sense to a Hindu, maybe even to a Buddhist or a Jain, but not to a Christian or a Muslim.

In Christianity and Islam, time is linear, beginning with descent from Eden and ending with a return to Heaven. Life on earth began after the Serpent tempted Adam and Eve to eat the Forbidden Fruit and will end when the Devil has been defeated and all souls return to their rightful place before God. In this understanding of the world, there is no notion of rebirth. The world does not repeat itself. There is one world, one life and only one chance. Thus the world view of Christians and Muslims is radically different from that of Hindus.

Scientists will refute both these notions of history. They will say these are religious beliefs, not mathematical facts. They will say there is no empirical proof of Treta yuga or Eden. They will demand that Hindus prove that Ram was actually born in Ayodhya and Ram actually built the bridge to Lanka. They will demand that Christians prove Jesus was actually born of a virgin and that Muslims prove Muhammad actually saw the angel Gabriel in the caves of Hira.

Such demands to legitimize beliefs through science are exercises in futility. They yield nothing but outrage, tension and violence. For religion is a matter of faith, not proof. Faith does not rely on reason; it speaks in a language that is indifferent to rationality.

Science and religion traverse different paths. Science explains how things happen—how does the sun rise and how are we born? Religion seeks to explain why things happen—why does the sun rise and why are we born? Science demands proof; religion seeks no validation.

Unfortunately, modern education systems have taught us to respect only that which can be proven empirically. Unless something is scientifically explained, we do not believe it is real. But experience tells us that some of the most profound ideas of humanity—God, soul, heaven, hell, ethics and morality—are not based on logic. Still, they have helped men become better human beings and establish mighty civilizations. Can concepts that have added such value to our lives be dismissed as mere superstitions?

Answers to religious questions are fundamentally cultural, not universal, as they are based on emotion. They are manmade constructs not natural phenomena; hence the parameters which define the answers to religious questions vary over history and geography. What was sacred in the past may not be so today. What is beautiful in one part of the world may not be so in another part of the world. Our notions of ethics have changed over time. Our ideas of appropriate social conduct have transformed with the world. Thus, what is correct to a Hindu may not be so for a Christian or Muslim and what makes sense to a Hindu, Christian or Muslim may not be so for a scientist or a historian.

The truth of a religion makes sense only to those who subscribe to it. For the rest, that truth may be falsehood. Thus religion anchors itself in myth—subjective truth of the believer, which is falsehood for the non-believer. Mythology is the vehicle of that truth—the stories, symbols and rituals that communicate the idea to the people through the ages. Myth expressed through mythology constructs the context for religion and faith. The idea of Ram makes little sense without belief in kalpas and rebirths just as the idea of Jesus and Muhammad makes little sense without the presupposition of the Original Sin and Fall of Man.

Failure or unwillingness to understand this very fundamental fact — that religion is anchored in subjective truth — is the basis of communal disharmony. Sometimes this failure or unwillingness to understand is sincere — it is lack of knowledge of a cultural belief which can be rectified through education and information. But often this unwillingness to grasp this basic concept is very deliberate and strategic, born of the desire to use religion as a tool for power.

Since the dawn of civilization, religion has been used for aggrandizing one group, and demonizing another. It is naïve to ignore the political side of religion.

Ram today has become a political icon of Hindutva, a new assertive manifestation of Hinduism that demands its place in the world's political history. Hindutva is a reaction to the traditional Hindu attitude of being tolerant and accommodating that many see as weakness.

The choice of Ram as a political icon over all the other forms of God described in Hindu scriptures is

Devdutt Pattanaik

significant. Being the obedient follower of rules, he is naturally much preferred over other manifestations such as Krishna, for example, who is the mischievous rule-breaking strategist, or Shiva, who is indifferent to worldly issues.

Ram, the political icon, sports muscles and has an aggressive stance—something that is not seen in religious iconography. Ram, the political icon, stands alone without his wife by his side—something that is unimaginable in sacred texts. Hindutva has gained power by transforming Ram into the symbol of Hindu pride, one who is ready to strike the enemy, quite different in character from the dignified and compassionate hero of the epics. At the same time, Hindutva's political opponents dismiss Ram as a poet's imagination which only alienates the devout Hindu.

This conflict, created by projecting Ram in a certain, partisan light, on one hand, or denying Ram's existence and significance altogether, on the other, has generated a powerful social and political dynamic that India cannot ignore.

But should Ram be seen only through the lens of those who use his name to justify rage or those who deny his value to the Hindu? Surely there is an alternative view of Ram, one that breaks the stranglehold of the politicians, one that focusses on the spiritual upliftment of humanity, not on the domination of one group over another? One must not forget that for centuries chanting Ram's name was supposed to calm the mind in times of stress, calamity or bereavement, reading the *Ramayana* was supposed to ensure harmony and order in the household; it is only since the twentieth century, since the politicization of Ram by one group and his rejection by another group, that Ram's name has been associated with anger, violence and tension.

Yes, Ram does raise his bow and kill Ravana. Many choose to interpret this as a licence to use violence against those whom they brand villains. Mythological tales must never be taken literally; they are symbolic, essentially containers of profound ideas. Ravana is killed not because he is evil or because he is Ram's political opponent. In keeping with the dominant theme of Vaishnava literature, Ram kills Ravana only because, despite being highly educated and extremely capable, Ravana stubbornly refuses to tame the animal within him, the animal that craves power and seeks to dominate. While such behaviour is appropriate for animals, it is not acceptable in humans. For animals it is matsya nyaya, law of the jungle, but for humans it is adharma, unrighteous conduct.

Ram is maryada purushottam, one who always upholds dharma. Dharma is not about controlling people or striking down the enemy. It is about looking beyond self-preservation and self-propagation. It is about caring for others, about loving and giving, not taking. It is about understanding people, accommodating people, making people feel secure and giving them a supportive environment. Dharma is about sacrificing desire with discipline on the altar of duty, about refusing to submit to the seductive passions roused by adharma, about outgrowing the animal within us. Dharma is what can transform a man into a god.

According to the *Adhyatma Ramayana*, Ravana is our ego, that part of us that is constantly seeking external validation. Having submitted to adharma, our ego has abducted Sita, our mind. That is why we constantly seek to dominate the world around us and that is why we do not accept it for what it is.

We have to rescue Sita. We have to unleash the power of Hanuman, our intellect, cross the sea of life, overpower Ravana, burn his golden Lanka and reunite Sita with Ram, who awaits discovery within us.

This Ram cannot be fettered to a particular period or a particular place. He is unbound by time and space. He exists everywhere at all times. He is our soul within us, our true identity, animating us, watching us.

When this Ram is realized, the desire for political victory ebbs. One is filled with love, wisdom and compassion for all. Dharma reigns supreme and Ram Rajya is established both within
and around us.

Devdutt Pattanaik

A Prayer to Ram

May Ram who is Raghu's descendant
protect my head,
May Ram who is Dashratha's son
protect my forehead,
May Ram who is Kaushalya's son
protect my eyes,
May Ram who is Vishwamitra's favourite
protect my ears,
May Ram who is the yagna's saviour
protect my nose,
May Ram who loves Lakshman
protect my mouth,
May Ram who is a sea of knowledge
protect my tongue,
May Ram who Bharata salutes
protect my neck,
May Ram who holds divine weapons
protect my shoulders,
May Ram who broke Shiva's bow
protect my arms,
May Ram who is Sita's husband
protect my hands,
May Ram who conquered Parashuram
protect my heart,

Devdutt Pattanaik

May Ram who killed the Rakshasa Khara
protect my abdomen,
May Ram who is Jambavan's refuge
protect my navel,
May Ram who is Sugriva's defender
protect my waist,
May Ram who is Hanuman's master
protect my hips,
May Ram who is the destroyer of the Rakshasas
protect my two thighs,
May Ram who built the bridge
protect my knees,
May Ram who killed the ten-faced demon
protect my shins,
May Ram who gave wealth to Vibhishana
protect my feet,
Thus may Ram protect my entire body

—From the *Rama Raksha Stotram* by
Buddhakaushika

Bibliography

- Bhattacharji, Sukumari. *The Indian Theogony*. New Delhi: Penguin Books, 2000.
- Coupe, Lawrence. *Myth*. London: Routledge, 1997.
- Dange, Sadashiv Ambadas. *Encyclopaedia of Puranic Beliefs and Practices*, Vols. 1–5. New Delhi: Navrang, 1990.
- Danielou, Alain. *Hindu Polytheism*. Rochester, Vt.: Inner Traditions International, 1991.
- Dodiya, Jaydipsinh K. *Critical Perspectives on the Ramayana*. New Delhi: Sarup and Sons, 2001.
- Flood, Gavin. *An Introduction to Hinduism*. New Delhi: Cambridge University Press, 1998.
- Frawley, David. *From the River of Heaven*. Delhi: Motilal Banarsidass, 1992.
- Hawley, J.S. and D.M. Wulff, eds. *The Divine Consort*. Boston: Beacon Press, 1982.
- Hopkins, E. Washburn. *Epic Mythology*. Delhi: Motilal Banarsidass, 1986.
- Jakimowicz-Shah, Marta. *Metamorphosis of Indian Gods*. Calcutta: Seagull Books, 1988.
- Kinsley, David. *Hindu Goddesses*. Delhi: Motilal Banarsidass, 1987.
- Klostermaier, Klaus K. *Hinduism: A Short History*. Oxford: Oneworld Publications, 2000.
- Knappert, Jan. *An Encyclopedia of Myth and Legend: Indian Mythology*. New Delhi: HarperCollins, 1992.
- Mani, Vettam. *Puranic Encyclopaedia*. Delhi: Motilal Banarsidass, 1996.
- Martin-Dubost, Paul. *Ganesha: Enchanter of the Three Worlds*. Mumbai: Franco-Indian Research, 1997.
- Menon, Ramesh. *The Ramayana: A Modern Retelling of the Great Indian Epic*. New York: North Point Press, 2004.

- Nagar, Shantilal. *Adbhut Ramayana*. Delhi: BRPC (India), 2001.
- ——. *Giridhar Ramayana*, New Delhi: Munshilal Manoharlal Publishers, 2003.
- Nath, Baij. *The Adhyatma Ramayana*, New Delhi: Cosmo Publications, 2005.
- O'Flaherty, Wendy Doniger, trans. *Hindu Myths*. Delhi: Penguin Books, 1975.
- ——. *Origins of Evil in Hindu Mythology*. New Delhi: Motilal Banarsidass, 1988.
- ——. *The Rig Veda: An Anthology*. New Delhi: Penguin Books, 1994.
- ——. *Sexual Metaphors and Animal Symbols in Indian Mythology*. New Delhi: Motilal Banarsidass, 1981.
- ——. *Siva: The Erotic Ascetic*. London: Oxford University Press Paperbacks, 1981.
- Pattanaik, Devdutt. *Devi: An Introduction*. Mumbai: Vakil, Feffer and Simons, 2000.
- ——. *Hanuman: An Introduction*. Mumbai: Vakil, Feffer and Simons, 2001.
- ——. *Indian Mythology: Tales, Symbols and Rituals from the Heart of the Indian Subcontinent*. Rochester, Vt.: Inner Traditions International, 2003.
- ——. *Lakshmi, Goddess of Wealth and Fortune: An Introduction*. Mumbai: Vakil, Feffer and Simons, 2003.
- ——. *Vishnu: An Introduction*. Mumbai: Vakil, Feffer and Simons, 1999.
- Richman, Paula (ed.). *Many Ramayanas: The Diversity of a Narrative Tradition in South Asia*. Berkeley: University of California Press, 1991.
- ——. *Questioning Ramayanas: A South Asian Tradition*. Berkeley: University of California Press, 2001.
- Saikia, Indira. *The Epic Hero in Campu Kavya*. Kolkata: Purthi Pustak, 2004.
- Sen, Makhan Lal. *The Ramayana of Valmiki*. Delhi: Munshiram Manoharlal, 1978.
- Singh, Avadhesh Kumar (ed.). *Ramayana Through the Ages: Rama-Gatha in Different Versions*. Delhi: D.K. Printworld, 2007.
- Toru, Ohnu. *Burmese Ramayana*. Delhi: BRPC (India), 1999.
- Walker, *Benjamin. Hindu World, Vols 1 and 2*. Delhi: Munshiram Manoharlal, 1983.
- Wilkins, W. J. *Hindu Mythology*. Delhi: Rupa, 1997.
- Zimmer, Heinrich. *Myths and Symbols in Indian Art and Civilization*. Delhi: Motilal Banarsidass, 1990.